The Final Message

A Roadmap to the book of Revelation

By

Robert R. Davis

Margie Ford!

I hope this book blesses
you as much as it has me.

Enjoy!

Robert

ISBN: 0-7596-9844-9 (softcover)
ISBN: 0-7596-9843-0 (ebook)

This book is printed on acid free paper.

1stBooks - rev. 3/27/02

Table of Contents

Introduction

Prologue

The Final Message is the result of my personal search for the true meaning behind the mystery of Revelation. No interpretation that I've read to date has left me with that "ah" feeling; the one you get when you realize you've finally found the truth or been enlightened. So I set out to satisfy my own hunger for the book's meaning and to share the results of my discovery. There are no overly complex charts or complicated theological explanations; I have purposely tried to get to the heart of the messages in the most direct manner possible.

I believe most times when we read Revelation we get so lost in the images, numbers, and the order of events, that we miss what God is saying to us. I know I did, I wanted to decipher every code and symbol in the book. Most times the only thing I got out of Revelation was frustration. But Revelation was written to help us, not to confuse or perplex us. John's prophecies will always attract scholars and laymen alike because of its apocalyptic nature.

The imagery in Revelation has many similarities to the book of Daniel. A major difference is that Daniel is meant to be a closed or sealed book, but Revelation is meant to be an open book (understood by its readers). When interpreting Revelation we must understand the myriad of Old Testament references and intricate system of biblical numbers. An isolated view of Revelation will never produce a true interpretation; it is imperative that we view it in light of the whole Bible.

Since Revelation is supposed to be understood by its readers, why did John use so many symbols? One reason is that words change their meaning over time but symbols and pictures are powerful forms of communication that can transcend generations. Also images can convey messages and spiritual truths that would otherwise be inexpressible in words. We have the saying "a picture is worth a thousand words"; such is the case with the book of Revelation.

Most people read Revelation to find out the cataclysmic events of the last days but they merely serve as background to God's main focus. The call of repentance is echoed throughout John's prophecies; salvation is the principle theme of Revelation. John portrays the Lord constantly reaching out to mankind throughout the pages of Revelation.

The book can be divided naturally into 3 separate parts. This division is given to us in the beginning of the book itself.

Revelation 1:19 Write the things which thou hast seen, and the things which are, and the things which shall be hereafter;

1. The things seen (Past)
2. The things which are (Present)
3. The things which shall be hereafter (Future).

Revelation is not just a foretelling of the end times, but it gives us a comprehensive view of the history of mankind from a heavenly perspective. It's the epic of battle for man's soul between the forces of good and evil from the Garden of Eden to Armageddon. Through John we have the unique privilege to get a behind the scenes look at the world past, present and future.

It is my sincere hope that after reading this book you will come away with a deeper appreciation and understanding of Revelation; along with a strong determination to persevere and receive the full riches of God's love. This book is not meant to be the end of your journey but it should lead you far enough so that you can continue confidently on your own.

John's Introduction
(Revelation 1)

The Revelation of Jesus Christ, which God gave unto him, to shew unto his servants things which must shortly come to pass; and he sent and signified *it* by his angel unto his servant John:

Who bare record of the word of God, and of the testimony of Jesus Christ, and of all things that he saw.

Blessed *is* he that readeth, and they that hear the words of this prophecy, and keep those things which are written therein: for the time *is* at hand.

Revelation 1:1-3

The very first thing John stresses in his letter is that these things will occur shortly. The purpose of stating that the time is near, it's so that we will stay in a state of perpetual readiness. For example if you wake up in the morning with an important meeting to go to you wouldn't lie around in your pajamas watching TV, unless of course you're one of my children. Instead you would get yourself prepared, groomed and ready to go. This is precisely what the writer is getting at, we need to be dressed and ready to go when Christ returns. The Lord has not given us the precise time of His return but He implores us to be ready.

*Matthew 24:36 But of **that day and hour knoweth no [man], no, not the angels of heaven, but my Father only.***
Matthew 24:37 But as the days of Noe [were], so shall also the coming of the Son of man be.

Even if the Lord doesn't come in our lifetime, we need to be ready because as the apostle James said "...For what is your life? It is even a vapor, that appears for a little time, and then vanishes away".[1] John wants to get our attention because the Lord (Christ) is coming. The event he is referring to, is the Second Advent or coming of Jesus. The first Advent of Christ was prophesied long before His arrival and some doubted that it would ever happen. The same is true with His Second Coming many doubt it's validity; never the less His Word is true.

John gives a salutation to the 7 churches that are in Asia. It is important to keep in mind when reading Revelation that John's writings were to strengthen these churches. If they could not understand his message how could they possibly gain comfort through it? Therefore in spite of the symbolism of the book the basic message of Revelation must have been understandable to the church at that time. Remember the church was going through a severe period of tribulation and persecution. John's words are meant to inspire, encourage and build up the churches. The same holds true for the church and people of this generation.

It is interesting to note the position of believers; they are considered kings and priests unto Christ and God. That is the position of every believer right now not in the after life. The word kings would be better understood as kingdom, we have been made into a kingdom of priests unto God. A priest in the Old Testament was a person that was set aside to minister (serve) God. They represented the people before God and offered various sacrifices for them. This office was regulated to the tribe of Levi and then only to the family of Aaron within the Levite tribe. Now the Lord has given this sacred office to every believer and commissioned us to reconcile the world unto God.

> *2 Corinthians 5:19 To wit, that God was in Christ, reconciling the world unto himself, not imputing their trespasses unto them; and hath **committed unto us the ministry of reconciliation**.*
>
> *2 Corinthians 5:20 Now then we are ambassadors for Christ, as though God did beseech you by us: we pray you in Christ's stead, be ye reconciled to God.*

Normally we would bypass John's introduction in order to get to the so-called deep parts of the prophecy. But God has placed a gem right under our noses. Every believer has an awesome responsibility before God, for we are His priests. Since the priest is the one who offers sacrifices and Christ is our eternal sacrifice, what do we offer to God?

> *Romans 12:1 ¶ I beseech you therefore, brethren, by the mercies of God, that ye **present your bodies a living sacrifice**, holy, acceptable unto God, which is your reasonable service.*

The picture that is presented here is a crucifying or mortifying of the flesh, denying or dying of self. This sacrifice is not for our sins (Christ has already taken care of that), we sacrifice ourselves in order to redeem (draw) others to Christ. This is our reasonable service or priestly duty, sacrificing ourselves to God for the sake (salvation) of others. No Christian can fulfill their sacred role as a priest without continually (daily) offering themselves as a living sacrifice.

A believer's personal conduct is of the utmost importance, not only do our actions affect others but they also are a determining factor in drawing people to God. Our daily conversation (conduct) is a far more effective witness than even our most compelling words. It is impossible to reconcile others to God, if we as priest do not offer the proper sacrifices (our bodies). This means sometimes forgoing our legitimate wants and needs in order to minister to the necessities of others.

In this first chapter of Revelation we also see that blessings are promised to those who read or hear this prophecy and are obedient to it. Over and over again the message is the same, repent! To repent simply means to feel regret for sin (s) and to change or turn away from them. As we begin to unfold John's prophecies we will see the myriad of blessings for turning to God (repentance) and the fatal consequences for not.

Now we come to the pivotal theme to Revelation, "Behold the Lord (Christ) is coming with the clouds". The Second Advent of Jesus is a major theme throughout John's prophecies. His first coming brought joy to the world but His return will bring mourning! Why such a contrast, isn't this the same Christ? His First Advent ushered in salvation to all that believed, His Second Coming will commence a time of judgment to all that don't.

Isaiah 13:9 Behold, **the day of the LORD cometh, cruel both with wrath and fierce anger,** *to lay the land desolate: and he shall destroy the sinners thereof out of it.*

2 Peter 3:10 But **the day of the Lord will come as a thief in the night;** *in the which the heavens shall pass away with a great noise, and the elements shall melt with fervent heat,* **the earth also and the works that are therein shall be burned up.**

The Second Coming will usher in an event called "the day of the Lord". But how will an event as big as the coming of Christ, come like a thief in the night? For nearly two thousand years the Church has cried He is coming; yes, but when? The reply is always soon; repent for the time is at hand. The result has been that people have fallen into a state of apathy. The call to repentance has become rhetoric, salvation seems needless and holiness is passé. We hear but we don't heed, we know but we don't act, it all seems so remote. Who really expects Christ to come right this minute and who is living as if He will? This is precisely why the day of the Lord will catch so many by surprise.

The Past

- **The Throne of God**
- **The Sealed Book**
- **The 7 Seals**
- **The 144,000 of Israel Sealed**
- **The Woman**
- **The War in Heaven**

Robert R. Davis

Chapter 1

The Throne of God
(Revelation 4)

After this I looked, and, behold, a door *was* opened in heaven: and the first voice which I heard *was* as it were of a trumpet talking with me; which said, Come up hither, and I will shew thee things which must be hereafter.

And immediately I was in the spirit: and, behold, a throne was set in heaven, and *one* sat on the throne.

And he that sat was to look upon like a jasper and a sardine stone: and *there was* a rainbow round about the throne, in sight like unto an emerald.

Revelation 4:1-3

Thishis is the second time John states that he was in the spirit, the first time he was in the spirit on the Lord's Day (Day of the Lord). John uses the term in the spirit on four different occasions, each time to denote a change in venue or time. Here John is moving from the earthly realm to the heavenly. First he sees an open door in heaven and then he is told to come up here (heaven). John is given access into heaven to see not only the things that will occur in the future (after 96 A.D.) but also the whole history of mankind from the spiritual perspective.

Through John's vision we too have the unique privilege to gain God's perspective on earthly events. The first thing John sees is the throne of God and His image seated upon the throne. Even in the spirit realm God's glory (true form) is too intense for John to bear. Therefore he is allowed only to see an image or representation of God.

The Lord is described as having the appearance of jasper and sardine (sardius) stone with an emerald rainbow over His throne. There is a purpose in using these 3 particular stones in connection to God and His throne.

The first stone mentioned is jasper, which in the Hebrew language literally means glittering; it is clear in color this speaks of God's glory, splendor and power. The second is sardine or sardius it is a blood red stone, this represents the life of or Spirit of God. So when John looked upon God, He was full of power (glory) and life. Lastly the emerald rainbow is a sign of the covenant between God, Noah and all creation.

We know the rainbow is a sign of the covenant but what is the significance of it being emerald in color. Green (emerald) typifies life in the earthly realm; signifying that the covenant is between God and all life. Additionally in the Old Testament the priest's breastplate had twelve stones, the 4th stone was emerald. Also in the book of Revelation itself the walls of Jerusalem were adorned with precious stones and the 4th stone again is emerald. Four is the number of creation or the world[2]. Therefore the emerald rainbow represents the covenant of God to all of creation. Oh, how intricate and detailed is the Word of God, with careful study we can clearly see this is not the work of many men but of one God.

Next our attention comes to the 24 elders, also seated on thrones around God. Who are these elders? They represent the 12 tribes of Israel and the 12 apostles of Jesus. These two entities share in the judgment of the world with God as indicated by their thrones, crowns and white robes. They also represent the separate dispensations by which mankind will be judged, the Old and New Testaments.

There are also 7 lamps of fire burning before God; John tells us that these lamps are the seven Spirits of God. In other words the lamps represent the Holy Spirit. Seven is the number of perfection or completion[3], so here we have the Spirit providing complete illumination to God. What is being inferred through this image is the Lord's omniscience.

In the 1st chapter of Revelation the Lord discloses to us that the seven lampstands represent churches. Naturally lamps go into lampstands, since lampstands represent the churches and the lamps represent the Holy Spirit. It is implied that the Holy Spirit belongs in the church to light its way or to give it direction. Also in the same verse are lightnings, thundering, and voices proceeding from the throne. This and the lamps of fire are indicative of the Holy Spirit. This is no different than saying the Holy Spirit, Holy Ghost, Spirit of God or the Comforter. Just as there are various names for the Holy Spirit, there are also many symbols for Him.

Also before the throne of God is a sea of crystal clear glass, waters or seas we are told by John represent multitudes and peoples[4]. This image depicts the whole world before God's throne. The fact that the sea is made of clear crystal points to the clarity in which God can into our lives. All that transpires in the earth is ever before Him and nothing escapes His view.

Now we come to the four living creatures full of eyes. The first like a lion, the second like a calf, the third had a face like a man and the fourth was like a flying eagle. This symbolism had stumped me for years; I always thought that they stood for all of creation before God, since four is the number of creation.

Compare the passages in Revelation chapter 4 with Ezekiel chapter 1 and Isaiah chapter 6, you will see that the 4 living creatures are the seraphim or cherubim. Most commentaries and bible dictionaries have them as two distinct creatures. Whether they are separate beings or the same, the question remains what are they and what is their purpose? The two in this instance are one in the same. The purpose of the seraphim or cherubim is to protect or watch over something. They represent a special type of angelic being but here they serve to represent the Holy Ghost, observe the following scriptures.

> *Ezekiel 1:13 As for the likeness of the living creatures, their **appearance was like burning coals of fire**, and like the **appearance of lamps**: it went up and down among the living creatures; and the fire was bright, and out of the fire went forth lightning.*

> *Ezekiel 1:14 And the living creatures ran and returned as the **appearance of a flash of lightning**.*

If you read the whole chapter from both Revelation (chapter 4) and Ezekiel (chapter 1) you will see that they are the same creatures. You will also see that they are describing the exact same scene in heaven. In Revelation we learn that the 7 lamps of burning fire, represent the Holy Spirit. In Ezekiel the creatures are like burning coals of fire and like lamps, clearly this yet is another description of the Spirit of God.

Note: that the seraphim or cherubim are not the Spirit of God but they serve only to describe His role in watching over creation as the eyes of God.

The 4 creatures continually cry out "Holy, Holy, Holy". This causes the 24 Elders to give God glory, honor and thanks. This is another indication that the four creatures are representative of the Spirit of God. So what we are actually seeing is the Holy Spirit, leading the elders into worship of the Lord. True worship only comes through the Spirit and inspiration of God. Jesus said, "God is a Spirit: and they that worship Him must worship Him in Spirit and in truth"[5].

Chapter 2

The Sealed Book
(Revelation 5)

**And they sung a new song, saying, Thou art worthy
to take the book, and to open the seals thereof: for thou
wast slain, and hast redeemed us to God by thy blood out
of every kindred, and tongue, and people, and nation;**

Revelation 5:9

Thre is a scroll in the right hand of God with writing on the front
and back sealed with 7 seals. A strong angel puts forth a
challenge, "Who is worthy to open the scroll and to loose its
seals?" No one in heaven or earth is found worthy to open the scroll or even
to look at it.

In scripture the right hand signifies power and strength. This is an
indication that no one can forcibly take the scroll but God must give it of
His own volition. He will only give the scroll to someone who is worthy but
who merits such high esteem in God's eyes? The scriptures tell us, "All
have sinned, and come short of the glory of God"[6]. In this vision the Lord
wants us to clearly see that Christ and Christ alone is worthy of this honor.
His life is a standard for all to follow and His selfless sacrifice upon the
cross qualifies Him for this unique privilege. It is also implied that if Jesus
had not prevailed to open the scroll that all of mankind would be doomed to
suffer the wrath of God due to their sin. But all thanks to God that through
Christ we can escape this horrible fate and experience the salvation of the
Lord.

In this vision Jesus is described as a slain lamb having 7 horns and 7
eyes. John tells us that the eyes are the seven Spirits of God (Holy Spirit)[7].
This implies that in Christ dwells the fullness of the Spirit, as indicated by
the number seven. The eyes of the Spirit see throughout the whole earth and
there is nothing that escapes His sight. Earlier we saw the Spirit as lamps
providing illumination to God; here we have the Spirit vigilantly observing
mankind.

The seven horns are mentioned but not really elaborated upon, horns in the book of Revelation represents kings or kingdoms. Seven as we mentioned earlier is the number of perfection or completion. The seven horns represent all of the kingdoms on the earth (the entire world), just as the seven lampstands represent the entire church. Since the horns are on the lamb, this tells us that they are under his control or power. We are very subtlety being told that Christ is ruling over the kingdoms of the world, what John is relating to us is prophetic since this has not happen yet.

> *Revelation 11:15 And the seventh angel sounded; and there were great voices in heaven, saying,* **The kingdoms of this world are become the kingdoms of our Lord, and of his Christ***; and he shall reign for ever and ever.*

Christ is reigning right now in the kingdom of God (the spiritual realm) and this kingdom will eventually overcome the kingdoms of the world (the earthly realm). As we can see from the above scripture this will not happen until after the seventh trumpet is sounded.

The main portion of this vision speaks of worshipping the Lamb because He was slain and redeemed us back unto God. In fact all those in heaven, earth, under the earth and in the seas are pictured worshipping the Lord (Christ). The crux of God's love for us is expressed in this one selfless act of passion. This is without a doubt the most important event in the history of mankind. The apostle Paul in the book of Philippians expressed it this way.

> *Philippians 2:8 And being found in fashion as a man, he humbled himself, and became obedient unto death, even the death of the cross.*
> *Philippians 2:9 Wherefore God also hath highly exalted him, and given him a name which is above every name:*
> *Philippians 2:10 That* **at the name of Jesus every knee should bow, of things in heaven, and things in earth, and things under the earth;**
> *Philippians 2:11 And that* **every tongue should confess that Jesus Christ is Lord***, to the glory of God the Father.*

The fact that everyone will confess that Jesus is Lord is not egotism on God's part. The word "Lord" in this application means one that is given great power or authority. Due to Christ obedience and death on the cross, God has bestowed upon Him great power and authority. The Bible is clear, everyone will acknowledge Christ's sacrifice; the question is will this confession cause you joy or remorse?

Chapter 3

The 7 Seals
(Revelation 6, 8:1-5)

1ˢᵗ Seal (White Horse)

> **And I saw, and behold a white horse: and he that sat on him had a bow; and a crown was given unto him: and he went forth conquering, and to conquer.**

> *Revelation 6:2*

To understand this image we must first interpret some symbols. White is the symbol for purity; it is never connected to evil in the book of Revelation. The bow is the symbol for victory; lastly the crown speaks of honor, power or dominion. What we have portrayed before us is the dominion given to Adam and Eve before the original sin. God gave mankind power and authority to rule over all of creation before the fall.

> *Genesis 1:28 And God blessed them, and **God said unto them**, Be fruitful, and multiply, and **replenish the earth, and subdue it**: and **have dominion** over the fish of the sea, and over the fowl of the air, and over every living thing that moveth upon the earth.*

Scripture tells us that in the beginning Adam and Eve were created as sinless (pure) beings with the freedom of choice. They were given dominion over the whole world; God's intention was that they would be the rulers over the earth. Every bird, fish and creature was to be in subjection to the authority of mankind. He was supposed to subdue or conquer all living things (except man himself) until everything was under his dominion. Of course man was to be under the authority of God but only God.

A conquering nature was put inside man from the beginning, in order for him to subdue the earth. It is for this reason that man today seeks to

9

climb the highest mountain, explore outer space and push himself to the limit. This nature was to be balanced with the Spirit of God within man. But when they fell (sinned) God's Spirit was removed and they died (spiritually). The balance was lost and the conquering nature became disproportionate.

When Adam and Eve lost their righteous standing before God, they gained an unwanted sinful nature through their disobedience. Consequently we have never realized the true potential that God has given to us to rule, due to sin man has forfeited his dominion over the earth. But God through His Son will subdue all powers and once again restore righteousness and dominion to the earth.

2nd Seal (Red Horse)

And there went out another horse that was red: and power was given to him that sat thereon to take peace from the earth, and that they should kill one another: and there was given unto him a great sword.

Revelation 6:4

Red is indicative of blood and in this image it symbolizes the spirit of murder or carnage. Although the Lamb is shown opening the seals in heaven, it's man through his disobedience who is actually unleashing this evil upon the earth. By transgressing against the commandment of God in the garden, Adam inadvertently opened up a type of Pandora's box. So it is man not God who is responsible for all the evil and wrong in the world today.

When Adam and Eve partook of the forbidden fruit from the tree of knowledge of good and evil, they introduced evil (sin) into the human experience. Knowledge applies to facts or ideas acquired by study, investigation, observation, or experience[8]. Prior to the original sin of mankind, evil was not a characteristic of humans. Afterwards of course we became quite familiar with it and all of its consequences. Sin or evil is now a part of the human makeup; through Adam man has become sinful by nature (I will explain why the sin nature is through Adam and not Eve in the 6th seal). Therefore all have sinned and come short of the glory of God. It doesn't matter how good or well behaved we are the problem is that we are now all spiritually impure (sinners) by birth.

We saw in the first seal that man was created pure but sin has perverted his original nature. There is no longer a restraint for his conquering spirit; man will not yield to anyone or anything. It is no longer our nature to submit to God but we are born fiercely independent even from our Creator.

The first seal was before the fall of man this one is afterwards. In the book of Genesis immediately after Adam and Eve sinned and were expelled from the garden the next debacle we see is the murder of Abel by his brother Cain. This is the first recorded manifestation of the 2nd seal in the Bible. Once this spirit of murder has been unleashed into the earth, it will remain until the end of the world and death itself is conquered.

3rd Seal (Black Horse)

And when he had opened the third seal, I heard the third beast say, Come and see. And I beheld, and lo a black horse; and he that sat on him had a pair of balances in his hand.

Revelation 6:5

In the Bible the color blacks implies sadness or want, in this instance it represents famines and scarcity throughout the earth. Shortages of food due to flooding, droughts, soil erosion, fires and pest have and will occur worldwide. This seal afflicts not just man but all creatures on the earth; this shows us that man's sin affects not only himself but also all of creation.

Even though famines will occur from time to time, man can alleviate most of the suffering that occurs from them. Even today thousands upon thousands die from starvation not because of the famine but because man will not open up his heart to his brother and share his resources. Governments deprive their own people of food for political motives; countries will not cooperate with their neighbors due to petty differences and squabbles.

This seal greatly affects the food sources of the world, resulting in devastating starvation across the world. We do not have the ability to end famines but we can minimize its effects if we act with compassion towards our fellowman. The suffering unleashed by this black horse is nothing in comparison to the devastation caused by our own dark hearts.

4th Seal (Pale Horse)

> **And I looked, and behold a pale horse: and his name that sat on him was Death, and Hell followed with him. And power was given unto them over the fourth part of the earth, to kill with sword, and with hunger, and with death, and with the beasts of the earth.**

> ***Revelation 6:8***

From the opening of this seal we see that man will experience physical death through a number of means. This 4th seal actually includes the first 3 seals with it to produce death over a fourth of the earth's population.

1. Sword - man killing man (2nd Seal)
2. Hunger - famines (3rd Seal)
3. Death - sickness, diseases and deterioration from aging (4th Seal)
4. Beasts of the earth - what man should have conquered (via the 1st Seal) now attack him.

Most of us are familiar with the horse of a pale color for it has traditionally symbolized death. What is the significance of Hell following Death? Hell represents separation from God, for wherever God dwells that is considered to be heaven. Separation from God is the ultimate penalty for sin, for God is life and to be apart from Him is death. Think of it this way, if the earth did not have the benefit of the sun, life would not exist. It is only because of our closeness to the sun that we are sustained.

It is not physical death that separates us from God, since only sin can disconnect us. The opening of the 4th seal has a two pronged effect upon the earth, first is physical death and the second is spiritual death (hell). Even though man has introduced death into the world by means of his sin, the biggest fear we need to address is how to escape the reality of hell (permanent separation from God).

Sin separates us from God and due to the fall of Adam, man is born with an innate sinful nature. Therefore it is normal or natural for us to sin, we will by our very nature commit sinful acts. It is because of this nature that we are disconnected from our creator. What we need is a way to reconnect us back to God and regain our sinless (original) nature.

5th Seal

And when he had opened the fifth seal, I saw under the altar the souls of them that were slain for the word of God, and for the testimony which they held:

Revelation 6:9

The first four seals dealt directly with creation, since four is the number of the world (creation). The number five represents incompleteness[9] and when this seal is opened we see that the time for God to avenge His saints has not yet been completed.

One thing that we should note is that the saints (Old Testament era) are under the altar of God, close to God but not truly with Him. This is because the price of sin (the sin nature) has not been paid at this point. Therefore all of the saints are separated from God until Christ comes to redeem mankind back unto the Lord. In spite of the righteous acts these saints have done for God, the law still binds them. For the law states that, "the wages of sin is death"[10] and also "the soul that sinneth it shall die"[11]. As we have already stated death is separation from God or rather eternal separation from Him. Obviously man stands in need of a savior, to rescue Him from the permanent effects of his sin.

The souls of those martyred for the Lord cry out unto Him to judge the world but they are told to wait a little while longer. Why, because before the Lord will judge the earth, He must extend salvation to the all flesh (Gentiles). Israel was called to be a peculiar nation, a nation of priest and God's chosen people. Through Israel the world was to see and know the true and living God. Instead of Israel influencing the other nations to follow after them and thereby lead them to God, they started imitating the ways of their pagan neighbors. But man through his sinfulness cannot frustrate the plans of God; the Lord placed a righteous seed in Israel to accomplish His will.

Jeremiah 23:5 Behold, the days come, saith the LORD, that I will raise unto David a righteous Branch, and a King shall reign and prosper, and shall execute judgment and justice in the earth.

Jeremiah 23:6 In his days Judah shall be saved, and Israel shall dwell safely: and this is his name whereby he shall be called, THE LORD OUR RIGHTEOUSNESS.

This prophecy states that the Messiah, the Son of God Himself, would come through the lineage of David and represent Israel in bringing salvation to the whole world. When Christ comes everyone will be able to walk in the light or revelation of God, for God has proclaimed that he is Lord over the whole earth and not just to the Jews.

The messianic prophecy is problematic because the souls under the heavenly altar are crying out for judgment and to be avenged of their enemies. The same was true on earth; Israel's hope was hinged upon the Messiah coming to bring judgment to the world and to establish His earthly kingdom. However Jesus' mission (1st Advent) was to bring salvation to all people and to establish God's spiritual kingdom in the earth. Only after the Second Advent of Christ will He establish His physical kingdom upon the earth.

The events of the day in Israel caused the people to focus only on the messianic prophecies that would bring them relief. This caused a distorted picture of the Messiah and His role in the minds of many Israelites. Consequently most in Israel did not recognize Jesus as the Messiah and they missed the very one they prayed so long for. Throughout history and even today people tend to view scriptures through current events and only highlight the parts that seem relevant. That is one of the primary reasons why there are so many wild theories and confusion over the book of Revelation today. We must insure that we look carefully at the whole prophecy that John is giving us, so that we too don't miss out.

6th Seal

> **And I beheld when he had opened the sixth seal, and, lo, there was a great earthquake; and the sun became black as sackcloth of hair, and the moon became as blood;**
>
> **And the stars of heaven fell unto the earth, even as a fig tree casteth her untimely figs, when she is shaken of a mighty wind.**

Revelation 6:12

Again we need to understand God images and symbols because the exact meaning of these passages is not obvious. The sun traditionally represents either God or Christ, in this particular scripture the sun represents God. The moon normally represents Israel or the church when used in the feminine sense. In this particular passage it points to Jesus in His earthly ministry; which is actually the formation of the church. We must keep in mind that the church is actually the body of Christ and He is the head. So the church is the incidental reference to the moon but Jesus is the true intent. John informs us that stars symbolize angels or leaders of the churches[12], in this case they represent literal angels.

What we see happening in this seal is not some cosmic future event but the actual crucifixion of Jesus Christ. There was a literal earthquake when Jesus was crucified. As for the sun becoming black as sackcloth of hair, sackcloth was used in times of mourning. God is shown here mourning the death (crucifixion) of His Son. In Matthew we see a physical representation of this with the sun being eclipsed for three whole hours. The moon became like blood, this is the actual death of Jesus upon the cross. The stars of heaven falling to the earth symbolize the angels under Satan's dominion losing their place in heaven after Christ's sacrifice for our sins. I will discuss the stars in heaven in greater detail when get to the "War in Heaven".

The last part of the chapter speaks of great fear in the people on the earth and of the impending wrath of God. At face value this looks to be the end of the age, but this cannot be because the 7th seal has not been opened. And the seventh seal ushers in the sounding of the 7 trumpets that have yet to be blown. So what is this scene? What we are viewing here is the wrath of God but to get the full understanding let's look at one of Jesus' parables.

> *Matthew 21:33 Hear another parable: There was a certain householder, which planted a vineyard, and hedged it round about, and digged a winepress in it, and built a tower, and let it out to husbandmen, and went into a far country:*
> *Matthew 21:34 And when the time of the fruit drew near, he sent his servants to the husbandmen, that they might receive the fruits of it.*
> *Matthew 21:35 And the husbandmen took his servants, and beat one, and killed another, and stoned another.*
> *Matthew 21:36 Again, he sent other servants more than the first: and they did unto them likewise.*
> *Matthew 21:37 But last of all he sent unto them his son, saying, they will reverence my son.*
> *Matthew 21:38 But when the husbandmen saw the son, they said among themselves, This is the heir; come, let us kill him, and let us seize on his inheritance.*

> *Matthew 21:39 And they caught him, and cast him out of the vineyard, and slew him.*
> *Matthew 21:40 **When the lord therefore of the vineyard cometh, what will he do unto those husbandmen?***
> *Matthew 21:41 **They say unto him, He will miserably destroy those wicked men**, and will let out his vineyard unto other husbandmen, which shall render him the fruits in their seasons.*

With the aid of this parable we can plainly see the reason for God's wrath. Israel represents the evil husbandman and God is the lord of the vineyard. Clearly we can see why God's wrath would be upon the house of Israel, they have rejected and killed His Son. What is not so clear is how the Gentiles (the world) fit into this picture.

> *St John 3:16 **For God so loved the world, that he gave his only begotten Son, that whosoever believeth in him should not perish, but have everlasting life.***
> *St John 3:17 For God sent not his Son into the world to condemn the world but that the world through him might be saved.*
> *St John 3:18 He that believeth on him is not condemned: but **he that believeth not is condemned already**, because he hath not believed in the name of the only begotten Son of God.*
> *St John 3:19 And this is the condemnation, that light is come into the world, and men loved darkness rather than light, because their deeds were evil.*

All who hear the gospel but do not believe in Christ and His work upon the cross are in fact rejecting Him. Israel's sin was that they rejected Jesus as the Messiah, subsequently all that do not believe in Him are guilty of the same. Therefore the world (both Jews and Gentiles) is depicted in this 6th seal as fearfully dreading the wrath of God to come. The Lord certainly knew that mankind would seek to kill His Son but He allowed it in order to redeem the world back unto Himself.

> **The reaction of God to the death of His Son should be the immediate destruction of man but instead He gives us grace. This is the true meaning of salvation.**

Here we see the Lord's love, patience and sovereignty. We can be sure of one thing, that God will exact His wrath upon all who reject His Son in His appointed time. So the last half of the 6th seal is a future prophecy that has yet to be fulfilled. In spite of man's actions the Lord has given us salvation (mercy) in place of His wrath.

Let's look briefly at why we need salvation in the first place. Salvation is not about how good you are or how well you follow the rules but with whom you choose to align yourself. There are some truly good people in the world and we wonder why they need to be saved or how can they possibly go to hell (separation from God).

Through physical birth we took on Adam's (sinful) nature and became separated from God. By spiritual birth (faith) we take on Christ's righteous nature and become reconnected to God. Being reborn or spiritual rebirth is an act of faith because it affects the spiritual (non-tangible) realm. We know that Jesus died on the cross for our sins (sin nature) and has reconnected us back to God through faith. But why was it necessary and how does this put us right with God?

The penalty for sin is death or separation from God. From the 2nd seal we learned that we are all sinful by nature through Adam. What is implied but not actually said is that our father's (man's) seed determines our sin nature. The sin nature of man (spiritual) is passed on from generation to generation; it is comparable to the father's chromosomes determining the sex of a child, while the mother remains neutral. This is why Jesus could be born of a human mother and yet is considered sinless.

Jesus became our substitute and took our sins (penalty for sins) upon the cross. This is why He cried out "My God, My God why have you forsaken (left) me"? The spirit of God actually departed from Jesus on the cross, when He took the sins of mankind upon Himself. Just as it happen with Adam after the fall, God removed His Spirit from Jesus. He experienced death (separation) for us, not just for a brief moment on the cross but for 3 whole days. Jesus remained dead physically and spiritually until His resurrection from the grave. <u>Christ suffered the horrors of hell, in order to keep us from experiencing it, that is the true depth of God's love for us</u>. Three is the number for completeness,[13] indicating that Christ paid the complete or total cost for our redemption.

17

Afterwards the Holy Ghost raised Him from the dead, clothed in a new resurrected body. This could only happen because Jesus was not paying for His own sins but ours. If we had to pay the penalty for sin in our own lives, there would be no justifiable reason to restore us back to life, since according to the law we truly deserved death.

God is not willing that we should die, He not only created us but He loves us. Instead Jesus took our place and paid the penalty in full. Since the penalty is death then we are considered dead and nailed to the cross of Calvary. That being the case the law has no jurisdiction over us since we are dead. The law pertains only to the living; it does not apply to those that are deceased. The crucifixion of Jesus has dealt with the issue of sin and death (the law) once and for all.

Once we're in Christ there's no issue of eternal separation (the law), since we're considered dead in Christ. Being in Christ also means that we have a new relationship with Him, God is now our Father. In this relationship if you sin (make a mistake), you simply asks for forgiveness just as you would with your natural (earthly) father. This is only possible through Jesus Christ because we are considered to be in Him or part of Him. So we now share in all of the blessings and privileges that Christ has in heaven and in earth. Does this mean that we can now sin without any grave penalties, since we are no longer under the law?

> *Hebrews 10:26 For **if we sin willfully** after that we have received the knowledge of the truth, **there remaineth no more sacrifice for sins.***

There are no loopholes in God, if we think that our new status in Christ gives us the liberty or license to sin we are deceiving ourselves. If we purposely continue to sin thinking God will forgive us afterwards, then we invalidate the sacrifice of Christ and we no longer have any exemption from the penalty of the law. We see in this seal that Christ has in His first coming restored our right standing before God. Later through His Second Coming He will complete all things and reestablish man's dominion over the earth.

We are all born as sinners (Adamic nature) that is an inescapable fact but through Jesus we have the privilege of determining our permanent relationship to God. Jesus died that we might have life but to experience that life we must accept (believe in) His Son. Knowing what we do about our sinful nature, how can we refuse the precious gift of salvation? The decision is yours; God will not force anyone to accept His Son.

7ᵗʰ Seal

And when he had opened the seventh seal, there was silence in heaven about the space of half an hour.

Revelation 8:1

We open this vision with a curious occurrence; there is silence in heaven for approximately a 1/2 hour. What causes confusion when reading the book of Revelation in sequential order is the insertion of the seventh chapter between the 6ᵗʰ and 7ᵗʰ seals. It is easier to understand the seals without trying to fit in the vision of the 144,000 Israelites and the great multitude of Gentiles from chapter seven. From what we have read and understood about the 6ᵗʰ seal, God was pictured mourning the physical loss of His Son. There is no actual break between the sixth and the seventh seals; the events in Revelation chapter 7 run parallel in time to this last seal.

Normally in heaven there is constant praise, honor and worship of God. Between the songs of the multitudes and the worship of the heavenly host heaven is never pictured as a quiet place. Silence indicates that something very serious must have happened or is happening. In the previous seal we saw the crucifixion or death of the Son of God. When the 7th seal is opened what we see is God (still covered in sackcloth - 6ᵗʰ seal) and all of heaven in a period of grieving over the physical death of Jesus.

*Lamentations 2:10 ¶ **The elders** of the daughter of Zion sit upon the ground, and **keep silence**: they have cast up dust upon their heads; **they have girded themselves with sackcloth**: the virgins of Jerusalem hang down their heads to the ground.*

We can see from the scriptures that in times of extreme grief it was customary to observe a period of silence. So significant is the death of Christ that all of heaven is silent, all worship and praise has ceased. Every heavenly being joins the Lord in silence to grieve over the loss of the only begotten Son of God. Obviously offering Jesus as a sacrifice for our sin was not a trivial matter to God.

After the grieving period is over, a time of comfort is necessary. This is what the incense and the prayers of the saints' represent. This offering is presented as a sweet aroma or pleasant fragrance before the Lord.

> **We see here that prayer has the ability to greatly move God; we then should give a high priority to our prayer life. We should pray the prayers that please God, prayers full of faith.**

After God has been comforted the angel fills his censer full of fire from the altar of God. Then he throws it to the earth and there were noises, thundering, lightning and an earthquake. We already established that these are symbols of the Holy Ghost. So what we see here is symbolic of the Holy Spirit being given to mankind (the day of Pentecost).

To the Jews Pentecost commemorates the law given by the Lord from Mt. Sinai on the fiftieth day out of Egypt. To the church it represents the day God wrote the law upon the hearts of men via the Holy Spirit.

> *Jeremiah 31:33   But **this shall be the covenant that I will make with the house of Israel**; After those days, saith the LORD, **I will put my law in their inward parts, and write it in their hearts;** and will be their God, and they shall be my people.*

Pentecost then is actually a continuation of the covenant made to Israel. Now it includes the Gentiles through Jesus into the inheritance of the descendants of Abraham. What God could not do through Israel because of their disobedient, He has accomplished with the death and resurrection of Jesus.

The covenant of God now extends to all of mankind through Christ by faith. The full blessing of God belongs to all that believe in His Son and not exclusively to Israel.

> **This new covenant has changed even our relationship from servants of God, to sons of God; this is truly the gospel (good news) of the kingdom.**

We have moved from death to life and from being slaves to sons, now everything that God has is ours but first we must confess with our mouths and believe in our hearts that Jesus Christ is Lord.

Chapter 4

The 144,000 of Israel Sealed
(Revelation 7:1-8)

Saying, Hurt not the earth, neither the sea, nor the trees, till we have sealed the servants of our God in their foreheads.
And I heard the number of them which were sealed: and there were sealed an hundred and forty and four thousand of all the tribes of the children of Israel.

Revelation 7:3,4

I n this vision we see the 144,000 of the children of Israel, commonly referred to as Jews. The reference to the Jews and the sealing of the 144,000 has been confusing to many because we did not fully grasp the meaning of the 6th seal. Everything in the book of Revelation from the 1st seal until now has been in sequential order, this event also happens before the 7th seal. The 144,000 were sealed on their foreheads with the seal of the living God, what exactly is this seal?

*Ephesians 1:13 In whom ye also trusted, after that ye heard the word of truth, the gospel of your salvation: in whom also after that ye believed, ye were **sealed with that Holy Spirit of promise**.*

The seal of God is the Holy Ghost. All who are God's are sealed with the Spirit to signify that they belong to Him. We also see God's use of numbers coming into play again. Twelve is the Lord's special number for His people; this includes all numbers that are multiples of twelve (144,000). Twelve speaks of permanent perfection, whereas the number seven represents dispensational (temporary) perfection. The number seven relates to this world, while twelve is connected to the heavenly realm. So, this sealing of the 144,000 is a permanent occurrence, never to be undone. I naturally thought that the 144,000 referred to the sealing of the Christian Jews of the early church.

The problem with that theory is that the 144,000 are also called the firstfruits of God and the Lamb. In the Old Testament the first fruits are gathered (harvested) and presented to God (in the temple) before the rest of the crop (harvest) is reaped. If 144,000 were the first converts of the early church, then they would have to be harvested before all of God's people are gathered (the rapture). We know from the Bible and historical record that this has not happened, so who are these Israelites from every tribe?

> *Matthew 27:52 And the graves were opened; and **many bodies of the saints which slept arose,***
> *Matthew 27:53 And came out of the graves **after his resurrection,** and **went into the holy city**, and appeared unto many.*

The firstfruits of the Lamb and God are actually the Old Testament saints and prophets. They were resurrected after Jesus rose victoriously from the grave and they presented themselves to God in the temple at Jerusalem (the holy city). These are the same ones (souls) we saw in the 5th seal under the altar of God. Only this time they are not just disembodied souls but now they have been clothed in their new resurrected bodies just like Christ. Until Jesus resolved the issue of sin and death, no one could receive the fullness of God's blessings. But now that Christ has paid the penalty of sin, these saints have been freed to enjoy true fellowship with God, no longer separated.

For eternal life is only through Christ, therefore until Jesus finished His work on the cross and was resurrected no one could experience God's eternal life. The law of sin and death bound everyone until this point but Jesus came to make us free (salvation) and to give us everlasting life. In order for man to truly experience eternal life, he must possess a body. Since man was designed in the image of God (the Trinity), he correspondingly is a three-dimensional being possessing a body, soul and spirit. Therefore he was not complete until Christ redeemed his new body, by satisfying the requirements of the law. In this vision we catch a glimpse of God's awesome plan of redemption.

Salvation was first offered to the Jews, then to the Gentiles (the rest of the world). This is the divine order and here we see the 144,000 are the firstfruits of the harvest, afterwards in the same chapter of Revelation we see the Great multitude of Gentiles that no one could count, this is the full harvest. They span from the early church until the end of this current dispensation, that being the case we will address them in detail later.

What a contrast between the 144,000 of Israel and the great multitude of Gentiles which no one could count, by comparison the Jews are only a fraction of the total harvest. The 144,000 is not a literal number but is meant to show that God has set aside a residue of Israel which will inherit His promises and in that number (twelve) we see the permanence of His election.

All of God's people are sealed upon their foreheads but in this vision only the firstfruits receive the seal. Remember that this vision starts concurrently with the 6th seal; at that time the Holy Spirit had not been given to all of mankind yet. The seal of the Holy Spirit is not only a sign of ownership but it is our guarantee or assurance concerning the future promises of God. Specifically the redemption of our bodies, Christ has already redeemed our souls but we are yet waiting to put on our new bodies. At the time of the rapture (the full harvest) death will have no more dominion over us and sickness will be a thing of the past and the curse of sin will be removed. This will be our eternal state in the kingdom of God.

Chapter 5

The Woman
(Revelation 12:1-6)

And there appeared a great wonder in heaven; a woman clothed with the sun, and the moon under her feet, and upon her head a crown of twelve stars:

And she being with child cried, travailing in birth, and pained to be delivered.

And there appeared another wonder in heaven; and behold a great red dragon, having seven heads and ten horns, and seven crowns upon his heads.

Revelation 12:1-3

The scriptures here portray a woman who is with child and a red dragon who is attempting to devour the young boy. The woman is clothed with the sun; here again the sun represents God. On her head is a garland with 12 stars, which we know stands for angels or leaders. In this instance the 12 stars point to the twelve tribes of Israel. She has the moon under her feet; once again the moon represents Christ. But do we have this right, is she walking or standing on Christ the Lord.

*Matthew 7:24   Therefore **whosoever heareth these sayings of mine, and doeth them, I will liken him unto a wise man, which built his house upon a rock:***

Matthew 7:25 And the rain descended, and the floods came, and the winds blew, and beat upon that house; and it fell not: for it was founded upon a rock.

*1 Corinthians 10:4 And did all drink the same spiritual drink: for they **drank of that spiritual Rock** that followed them: and **that Rock was Christ.***

From these scriptures we can see that Christ is our rock or foundation, for He is the Word become flesh. So the reference to the Lord being under the woman's feet is totally valid. With all of these pieces in place we can see that the woman represents the earthly kingdom or nation of Israel. Therefore the child that she birthed was the Messiah, Jesus Christ the Lord. The dragon that opposes the Christ child is Satan, whose identity is given to us later by John. The devil literally tried to devour the child as soon as He was born.

> *Matthew 2:13 ¶ And when they were departed, behold, the angel of the Lord appeareth to Joseph in a dream, saying, Arise, and take the young child and his mother, and flee into Egypt, and be thou there until I bring thee word: for* **Herod will seek the young child to destroy him.**
> *Matthew 2:14 When he arose, he took the young child and his mother by night, and departed into Egypt:*
> *Matthew 2:15 And was there until the death of Herod: that it might be fulfilled which was spoken of the Lord by the prophet, saying, Out of Egypt have I called my son.*
> *Matthew 2:16 ¶ Then* **Herod, when he saw that he was mocked of the wise men, was exceeding wroth, and sent forth, and slew all the children that were in Bethlehem, and in all the coasts thereof, from two years old and under,** *according to the time which he had diligently enquired of the wise men.*

I am not inferring that Herod was Satan or the he represents the devil. He was merely the vehicle that Satan used to accomplish his goals, Herod allowed himself to be influenced to do wrong. We are all susceptible to being wrongly influenced; this is why we need the Spirit of God in us to give us guidance in our daily lives. Anyone without God's spirit is vulnerable to the whims of Satan. Everyone can see the hand of Satan in people who commit great atrocities; we can't fathom how people can be so cruel or evil. We tell ourselves that we could never do such things and fool ourselves into thinking that we're all right. By focusing on the faults of others we never see all of the little ways in which we ourselves are being influenced. This is how Satan deceives us into becoming unwitting participants into his many schemes.

When John views this event he declares that it is a great wonder in heaven. The book of Revelation is full of signs and symbols, so why is this event singled out and called a great wonder (sign)?

*Isaiah 7:14 Therefore the **Lord himself shall give you a sign; Behold, a virgin shall conceive, and bear a son,** and shall call his name Immanuel.*

Never before in history and never again to be repeated, shall a virgin give birth without the seed of a man. God sent his only Son into the world to redeem mankind back unto Himself. No miracle that has ever been performed can even come close to what was done through Christ. Even today we are still experiencing the life changing effects of this miraculous sign.

Satan cannot duplicate this sign because there is no life in him; the Spirit of God alone is the world's life giving force. If Satan had the ability to impregnate a woman, he would have done so long ago. He wouldn't be waiting on God's appointed time because he has his own agenda for the world. Would the devil stop at producing one child (the infamous antichrist)? I believe that he would produce an army of them to wreck havoc in the world. From this we can see yet another reason why the virgin birth is considered such a great sign in heaven; because it can never be duplicated.

Next the dragon throws a third of the stars to the earth, stars we know are angels or leaders but I believe that this time they are real or literal angels. These angels are Satan's demonic host, those who have followed him in rebellion against God. They are cast down to the earth because as we shall see shortly Satan himself has been cast down. Here we see another great sign in heaven; I believe that we can better understand this sign when we look at the "War in Heaven". Lastly the woman (Israel) flees to the desert and is taken care of for 1260 days, I will address that when we come to the "Two Witnesses".

Chapter 6

The War in Heaven
(Revelation 12:7-12)

And the great dragon was cast out, that old serpent, called he Devil, and Satan, which deceiveth the whole world: he was cast out into the earth, and his angels were cast out with him.

Revelation 12:9

Now we can definitely see that the stars the dragon threw to earth were literal angels. John alluded to this event in the 6th seal but the true meaning of it wasn't introduced until the 12th chapter of Revelation. At one time Satan and his angels had positions in heaven. But when they lost the fight with Michael, their place was no longer found in heaven. We are not told what started this war but we are told of how it ends. Satan and his angels lose the war against Michael and his angels. Who is Michael and what is his position?

Daniel 10:12 Then said he unto me, Fear not, Daniel: for from the first day that thou didst set thine heart to understand, and to chasten thyself before thy God, thy words were heard, and I am come for thy words.
*Daniel 10:13 But the prince of the kingdom of Persia withstood me one and twenty days: but, lo, **Michael, one of the chief princes**, came to help me; and I remained there with the kings of Persia.*

Michael is a prince over the angels of God; angels are ministering spirits that work on our behalf. Later, John tells us that they are our fellow brethren and they are not to be worshipped.

27

Robert R. Davis

> **Note: We can also derive from Daniel 10 that angels both angelic and demonic are setup over regions or territories in the earth.**

What is significant, is not the fact that Michael's angels won we would expect that outcome. But what's really important here is how they won; they overcame Satan by the blood of the Lamb and the word of their testimony. This is of major importance to us for two reasons. 1) Since Satan has been cast to earth he will make war with us (Christians). 2) The weapons that the angels used are at our disposal.

They applied the blood of the Lamb; to do this we must be His disciples. The blood of Christ cleanses us from every sin; we apply it initially by confessing that Jesus is Lord of our lives. After this point the blood is applied to our subsequent sins by confessing them to the Lord. They also used the word of their testimony, this is not testifying or our own personal testimonies. For what testimony would the angels of heaven have about God in their lives? Testifying is something you do to edify the body of Christ (build up other Christians) not to defeat Satan. What then is the meaning of the "word of our testimony"?

> *Exodus 25:21 And thou shalt put the mercy seat above upon the ark; and **in the ark thou shalt put the testimony that I shall give thee**.*

The testimony is the Word of God, we see in Exodus the stone tablets (the Ten Commandments) being put into the ark. So the Word of our testimony refers to us declaring God's Holy Word. Even Jesus Himself used this important weapon to defeat Satan, when He was tempted in the wilderness.

Notice in every temptation Jesus said, "it is written", if He quoted the Word of God. Surely we cannot hope to defeat Satan without it. Christ has given His saints the key (authority) to overcome Satan, demons and spiritual strongholds (territories under demonic control) through His blood and the Word of God.

> **Note: The keys to overcoming Satan and the flesh.**
> **1. The blood of the Lamb - Believing.**
> **2. The Word of our Testimony - Confessing.**

As we mentioned earlier there was another great sign in heaven, an enormous red dragon with 7 heads and 10 horns each head having a crown. We have already established that Satan is the dragon. The seven heads represent 7 great kingdoms in the earth and the 10 horns are future kingdoms yet to be established. Together they represent the world's kingdoms or the kingdoms of man. Satan is currently ruling the kingdoms of the world; he has stolen this authority from Adam through his disobedience. But how did Adam's sin cause this to happen?

> *Romans 6:16* **Know ye not, that to whom ye yield yourselves** *servants to obey,* **his servants ye are to whom ye obey;** *whether of sin unto death, or of obedience unto righteousness?*

In other words when Adam obeyed the voice of Satan through Eve, he became the servant of Satan. A servant or slave does not have authority even over his or her body but everything they have becomes the property of their master. All prior rights and powers are transferred to the owner. If Adam had obeyed God, nothing would have been lost since it was God who gave him the authority over the earth in the first place. But when Adam listened to the voice of Satan via his wife, the devil immediately confiscated his belongings (authority) and began to rule over him.

The visible sign that Satan has been cast down is the power and authority given to us through Jesus Christ, because Satan's fall is a spiritual reality that cannot be seen with the human eye. The fact that the saints of God posses this new power and authority is indicative of Satan being removed from his place. Now the kingdom of God has truly come and Christ has given the keys to the kingdom to his church.

> *Luke 10:17* ¶ *And the seventy returned again with joy, saying, Lord, even the devils are subject unto us through thy name.*
> *Luke 10:18* *And he said unto them,* **I beheld Satan as lightning fall from heaven.**
> *Luke 10:19* **Behold, I give unto you power** *to tread on serpents and scorpions, and* **over all the power of the enemy:** *and nothing shall by any means hurt you.*

So the tangible proof that Satan has been cast down to the earth, is the power of the kingdom given to the people of God. The book of Matthew puts it this way.

> *Matthew 16:17 And **these signs shall follow them that
> believe**; In my name shall they cast out devils; they shall
> speak with new tongues;*
> *Matthew 16:18 They shall take up serpents; and if they
> drink any deadly thing, it shall not hurt them; they shall lay
> hands on the sick, and they shall recover."*

Even though Satan has been cast down to the earth, he is still the ruler or master of this present world (through default). His power in the earth has not been taken away but the saints have been given authority to destroy all the works of the enemy. The devil is furious and will stop at nothing to conquer the children of the kingdom. So when you decide to make your peace with God, you are automatically declaring war with the devil. But thank God that he has given us the victory over every work of the enemy through Christ Jesus. For we overcome through the blood of the Lamb and the Word of our testimony.

The Present

- **The War on Earth**
- **The Two Witnesses**
- **Satan Bound a 1,000 Years**
- **Saints Reign a 1,000 Years**
- **The Revelation of Christ**
- **The 7 Letters**
- **The 7 Trumpets**
- **The Beast out of the Sea**
- **The Beast out of the Earth**
- **The Announcements of the 3 Angels**
- **The Little Book**

Robert R. Davis

Chapter 7

The War on Earth
(Revelation 12:13-17)

And when the dragon saw that he was cast unto the earth, he persecuted the woman which brought forth the man *child*.

And the dragon was wroth with the woman, and went to make war with the remnant of her seed, which keep the commandments of God, and have the testimony of Jesus Christ.

Revelation 12:13,17

T he dragon once he realized that he lost his place in heaven and was cast down to the earth began to persecute the woman (Israel). But Israel was given two wings to fly away into the wilderness to be nourished, away from the serpent (devil). How can this be because we know that Israel has been persecuted throughout its history? Notice also that the serpent spit out water like a flood after the woman, that the flood might carry her away.

> *Daniel 11:22 And **with the arms of a flood** shall they be overflown from before him, and shall be broken; yea, also the prince of the covenant.*

The flood speaks of a mighty force, specifically an army. When the Roman army destroyed Jerusalem in 70 A.D. the Jews fled into the wilderness. The wilderness is any place that is not the physical territory or state called Israel. So how is Israel away from Satan being fed or nourished? This point's to the fact that Israel has been growing or rebuilding while the church fulfills its role. It took almost 1900 years but Israel has become a state or nation again.

Satan knows and understands prophecy, he understood that Israel was being nourished (rebuilding) to one day become a nation again. Just as he tried to stop (kill) the Messiah from being born, he has attempted to abort the rebirth of Israel. Israel became a nation or state again in 1948. Just before that time the Nazi's killed approximately 6 million Jews (the Holocaust) during World War II (1939 - 1945). This was an obvious attempt to stop the prophecy of Israel's rebirth from being fulfilled.

Since Satan could not destroy the woman (Israel) before she birthed the Messiah, he has declared war against the rest of her offspring, the church. Every war has a name; the bible calls it "The Great Tribulation". Many believe that the church will not be involved in the great tribulation and that it is yet a future event. So lets examine the tribulation to see if the church is involved or not.

First what is tribulation, the word means great affliction, trial or distress[14]. It is suffering resulting from persecution, literally it means to drag or throw down. It is called the great tribulation because of its magnitude and duration, the same as America's great depression in the early 1900's. From that definition we could conclude that the church fits into the category of the great tribulation but let's see what the Bible says about the subject.

*Acts 14:22 Confirming the souls of the disciples, and exhorting them to continue in the faith, and that we must through **much tribulation enter into the kingdom of God**.*

*Acts 8:1 And Saul was consenting unto his death. And at that time there was a **great persecution against the church** which was at Jerusalem; and they were all scattered abroad throughout the regions of Judaea and Samaria, except the apostles.*

Clearly the Bible teaches us that through much or great tribulation we will enter into the kingdom of God. Also, history lets us know that the church has through the years gone through great persecution. Most of the overt physical persecution of the church doesn't exist in America today and that has unfortunately lulled her into a misconception that she is not under attack. Do not be fooled the kingdom of God and the kingdoms of this world are diametrically opposed to each other.

> *Genesis3:14 ¶ And the LORD God said unto the serpent, Because thou hast done this, thou art cursed above all cattle, and above every beast of the field; upon thy belly shalt thou go, and dust shalt thou eat all the days of thy life:*
> *Genesis 3:15 And **I will put enmity between thee and the woman, and between thy seed and her seed;** he shall bruise thy head, and thou shalt bruise his heel.*

This passage of scripture is commonly known as the first prophecy concerning the coming of the Messiah (Christ). God placed enmity between the serpent (devil) and the woman through Christ. That being the case the woman described cannot be Eve, because the hostility would have to end when Eve died. The woman here also refers to Israel and again her seed is Jesus and the church.   Satan's seed is anyone outside the church (unbelievers).

There will always be enmity between Satan's seed (unbelievers) and the woman's seed (believers). Coupled with the fact that Satan rules this present world, how can we experience anything but extreme tribulation and persecution?

Notice that Satan will bruise his (man's) heel, which literally means that he will supplant man. This has already happened as we have seen; he has replaced man as the ruler of the earth.

But the other part of the prophecy was fulfilled through Jesus, he (Christ) shall bruise your head (Satan). The head represents rulership, so the work of Christ directly affects the dominion of Satan. First Jesus died for our sins paying the penalty of the law and then He was resurrected into the newness of life. After His resurrection He gave every believer full authority over the power of the enemy, bruising the head of the enemy. Whenever a Christian uses their authority over the adversary his dominion is weakened. When the kingdoms of this world become the kingdoms of our Lord, then Christ will totally crush the head of Satan. The fate of Satan is sealed and the Lord's victory is sure but it is imperative that we fight the good fight of faith in order to overcome our adversary.

Chapter 8

The Two Witnesses
(Revelation 11:1-14)

And I will give *power* unto my two witnesses, and they shall prophesy a thousand two hundred *and* threescore days, clothed in sackcloth.

Revelation 11:3

W e have here the mystery of the two witnesses. Much speculation has evolved concerning their true identity. The Bible leaves clues to help determine who they are. They are also described as two olive trees and as the two anointed ones that stand before God.

> *Zechariah 4:11 ¶ Then answered I, and said unto him,* **What are these two olive trees** *upon the right side of the candlestick and upon the left side thereof?*
> *Zechariah 4:12 And I answered again, and said unto him,* **What be these two olive branches** *which through the two golden pipes empty the golden oil out of themselves?*
> *Zechariah 4:13 And he answered me and said,* **Knowest thou not what these be?** *And I said, No, my lord.*
> *Zechariah 4:14 Then said he,* **These are the two anointed ones, that stand by the Lord of the whole earth.**

It is said that these two stand by or before God; earlier in the book when we discussed the throne of God. We saw before the throne, 24 elders and 4 living creatures. The creatures we said represented the Holy Spirit over all of creation. Due to the bible's use of numbers the Spirit of God does not really fit as the two witnesses. We stated that the 24 elders represented both Israel and the church; these 2 entities stand before God at all times. The church consisting of both Jewish and Gentile believers represents the 2 witnesses. It should be noted that when we refer to Israel as one of the two witnesses, we are speaking only of the Jews within the church (Christian Jews). They are the remnant of the house of Israel that God has saved and they are in fact representing the entire house of Israel. Israel's number the 144,000 has been sealed or closed with the resurrection of Christ. All Jews after this point are included in the church, the dispensation of grace. But why make distinctions within the church; it would be better to think of the church, as just one witness wouldn't it?

> *Deuteronomy 19:15 One witness shall not rise up against a man **for any iniquity, or for any sin**, in any sin that he sinneth: **at the mouth of two witnesses**, or at the mouth of three witnesses, **shall the matter be established.***

This particular passage shows us clearly why God has chosen to have 2 witnesses (Israel and the Church). If we fail to heed the voice of God and yield ourselves to Him, then these witnesses will stand to condemn us. Actually Israel and the church are living representations of both the Old and New Testaments respectively. They are to publish (spread) or preach the gospel throughout the entire world. So in actuality it is by the Word of God that we are judged and it stands eternally as God's faithful witness. The Lord has set these 2 witnesses before us, so that we may chose either life or death. Our final destination is totally in our hands, God has given us the responsibility to choose.

Next there are several numbers we must deal with in order to understand what's happening with the church's ministry. The Gentiles will tread Jerusalem under foot for 42 months. The two witnesses (the church) will prophesy 1260 days. After their ministry is completed they will be killed and lay unburied for 3 ½ days. If we look closely we will see a pattern, all the numbers equate to 3 ½ units.

Note: you must use the Jewish calendar to calculate this; their year has only 360 days.

Divide 1260 days by 360 days (1 year) the result is 3 ½ years. Likewise if you divide 12 months into 42 months the result is 3 ½ years. What then is the significance of this number?

Some believe that this is the 70th week spoken of in the book of Daniel but that prophetic week was fulfilled with the destruction of Jerusalem. What's really happening here is that Jesus is giving power to His 2 witnesses, (the Church) to fulfill their ministry.

Robert R. Davis

The ministry of the church is the same as the ministry of Christ. The church is the body of Christ, with Jesus as the head of course. This concept is reinforced by the length of time the church has to minister. Jesus ministered for 3 ½ years while on earth, the 2 witnesses time to prophesy is exactly the same length of time. Jesus was in the grave (dead) for 3 ½ days; again the witnesses will lay dead for the same time span. Through this parallel we see that the church's mission is to fulfill the ministry of Christ. Before we move on lets first establish that Jesus was dead for 3 ½ days, because this goes against our traditional beliefs.

Contrary to popular belief Jesus did not die on Good Friday; if He did then it would be impossible for Him to be in the grave for 3 days. The scriptures clearly state that he rose on the first day of the week (Sunday). What causes confusion is the use of the term Sabbath, the seventh day or the Sabbath is Saturday (actually Friday 6:00pm - Saturday 6:00pm). There are certain Jewish holidays or holy days that are considered Sabbaths these are also called high days; the Passover is one of those days. In the Jewish tradition the day starts at 6:00 pm and ends the next evening at the same time. Based on the gospels this is an approx timeframe for Jesus' death and resurrection, which comes out to be approx. 3 ½ days.

Day 0
    Tuesday 6:00pm - Wednesday 6:00pm
    Preparation Day for the Passover
    Jesus is crucified approx. 9:00am (Wednesday morning)[15]
    Jesus dies approx. 3:00pm (Wednesday evening)[16]
    Jesus is buried between 3:00pm - 6:00pm
Day 1
    Wednesday 6:00pm - Thursday 6:00pm
    Sabbath (Passover)
Day 2
    Thursday 6:00pm - Friday 6:00pm
Day 3
    Friday 6:00pm - Saturday 6:00pm
    Sabbath (Actual)
Day 4
    Saturday 6:00pm - Sunday 6:00pm
    Christ Resurrected Sunday 3:00am - 6:00am (approx. timeframe)[17]

Now that we've established the timeframe of Jesus' death, let's go back to our numbers, 42 months and 1260 days. We also see that the Holy City is being tread under foot for 42 months, this also equates to 3 ½ years. The length of the church's testimony or ministry is 1260 days, which equates to 3 ½ years. Remember in John's vision of "The Woman", we saw that Israel was going to the wilderness for 1260 days. Now we can see that all of these occurrences are referring to the same period of time.

Now we are ready to deal with our vision of the 2 witnesses again, the church has a specific time frame to prophesy (3 ½ years). The reference to sackcloth here denotes a call to repentance; referring to the practice of the prophets from the Old Testament era. At the end of the church's ministry, it is overcome and killed the same as Jesus. How can this be? Remember we are talking about the church and not individuals.

The church cannot physically die and it certainly cannot die spiritually as long as Christ is the head. Then what does this reference mean? The church will no longer be a strong moral influence in our government or society. So the church or churches will physically exist as they always have only their power to influence will be gone (killed). The world is happy to be rid of the churches moral codes and restrictions; this is what the reference is pointing when it says the inhabitants of the earth are celebrating the death of the 2 witnesses.

After 3 ½ days the church (2 witnesses) will be restored to life again, just like Jesus. This is an implication to a revival period within the church, so that it regains its influence upon society again. At this point we are presented with another concept. A voice from heaven says, "Come up here" and the church (2 witnesses) ascends to heaven in a cloud, for all to see.

The church commonly calls what we are dealing with here the rapture. The term rapture is not actually used in the Bible; it would be more proper to refer to it as the resurrection. Remember we said the church is fulfilling the ministry of Jesus and after 3 days (actually 3 ½) in the grave he arose or was resurrected. Jesus told His disciples to pick up their crosses and to follow Him; we see here that the church is to literally follow Christ in every way.

We will deal with the subject of the rapture in more detail later when we discuss the "Harvest Judgment". After the rapture a tenth of Jerusalem falls via an earthquake, 7,000 were killed; those left gave glory to God. This too must be a sign to the people of the earth; unfortunately reacting to this sign will be a little too late, since the rapture has already occurred.

Let's digress for a moment and review some facts. The 2 witnesses time to prophesy, the holy city (Jerusalem) being given to the Gentiles and the woman (Israel) fleeing into the wilderness all occur simultaneously. We can now put a few things in perspective; in 1948 Israel became a nation once again. Signifying that the woman (Israel) is no longer in the wilderness and the holy city is no longer given over to the Gentiles. This would also mean that the time for the church to prophesy ended in 1948, meaning their strong influence over the world has been destroyed.

Could this be true has the church's power really been limited? Look at any country that is predominately Christian and evaluate their current moral condition. Take the United States as a prime example and look at the changes that have occurred since 1948. Many Christians today cannot understand why the church doesn't seem to make any headway when combating various moral issues. But this makes sense when we understand the prophecy that John has given to us.

Thankfully this period is much shorter (3 ½ days as opposed to 3 ½ years) than the first one. So at this point although the church is dead, she is waiting on the breath of life from God (revival and resurrection). With this in mind every Christian (the church) should be in a posture of prayer and fasting as we wait on God's next move. After the 2 witnesses are revived, then the Lord will come for His church (the rapture). This will end the period of grace (church era) and usher in the wrath of God.

The next visible sign will be the rapture of the church, as we said before if you're able to see this, then you've already missed out. We need to be more serious now than ever before about our faith, since there are no more signs left before the resurrection. If we miss this opportunity then we must endure the wrath of God (Day of the Lord). At that point God's Spirit and the church will be removed from the earth, which will cause an exponential increase of evil in the world. Satan's full power will be unleashed since the hindrance of the church will be gone.

Who will be able to stand in such an hour? It cannot be overstated; the time for salvation is now!

Chapter 9

Satan Bound a 1,000 Years
(Revelation 20:1-3)

And I saw an angel come down from heaven, having the key of the bottomless pit and a great chain in his hand.

And he laid hold on the dragon, that old serpent, which is the Devil, and Satan, and bound him a thousand years.

And cast him into the bottomless pit, and shut him up, and set a seal upon him, that he should deceive the nations no more, till the thousand years should be fulfilled: and after that he must be loosed a little season.

Revelation 20:1-3

John is of course being very figurative in his descriptions. In the second verse he uses four different names to describe Satan. The titles serpent and dragon tells us that he is a deceiver both in the Old and New Testaments respectively. The name Devil means liar and we know he is the father of lies and lastly the term Satan signifies that he is our enemy or adversary. So how exactly do we bind our lying enemy from deceiving the nations? With the truth that's how, what else can stop a lie except the truth?

*John 14:6 **Jesus saith** unto him, **I am** the way, **the truth**, and the life: no man cometh unto the Father, but by me.*

*John 14:16 And I will pray the Father, and he shall give you another **Comforter**, that he may abide with you for ever;*

*John 14:17 [Even] **the Spirit of truth**; whom the world cannot receive, because it seeth him not, neither knoweth him: but ye know him; for he dwelleth with you, and shall be in you.*

We know from the scriptures that Jesus is the truth and the Holy Spirit that seals us and abides within is called the Spirit of Truth. So in practical terms the truth is the revelation or presentation of the gospel of Jesus Christ. It is through the preaching, teaching and obeying of the gospel that Satan is bound. This makes practical sense but is there any scriptural backing to support this theory?

> *Matthew 12:28 But if I cast out devils by the Spirit of God, then the kingdom of God is come unto you.*
> *Matthew 12:29 Or else how can one enter into a strong man's house, and spoil his goods, **except he first bind the strong man?** and then he will spoil his house.*

In this parable the strong man is Satan, his house is the kingdom of this world and the goods represent mankind. Jesus is telling us that the only way that He can cast out devils is by first binding Satan. As we discussed earlier in the "War in heaven" one of the signs of the believer is casting of devils (Matthew 16:17-18). Since every believer has the power to cast out devils, then Satan has already been bound.

Yet we know that Satan is still wrecking havoc in the earth, so how exactly is he bound? The devil is a spirit therefore he cannot be physically tied to a chain or anything else for that matter. The reference to binding Satan means to constrain with legal authority. Jesus had legal authority over Satan when He dwelt on earth, just as He did in heaven. Man however lost his authority through sin; Christ has regained it for man by His sacrifice on the cross and gives it freely to those who follow Him.

> *Matthew 16:19 And I will **give unto thee the keys of the kingdom** of heaven: and **whatsoever thou shalt bind on earth shall be bound in heaven**: and whatsoever thou shalt loose on earth shall be loosed in heaven.*

Every citizen of the kingdom of God has the legal authority to bind and loose on the earth. We can bind the works and activities of the devil and loose all those who have been imprisoned by him. For example in the area of healing if you loose someone through the laying on of hands from a particular sickness or disease, the devil is powerless to resist without the person's consent. Consent would take the form of unbelief or inadequate faith but when faith is applied to the Word of God, Satan is truly bound.

As far as Satan not being able to deceive the nations anymore for 1000 years, the gospel message is unique to the law. Prior to Jesus the law was not published and proclaimed throughout the world. Israel received the law directly from God and it was given only to them. Other nations were supposed to see how blessed Israel was and start to follow after them. Attributing Israel's great success and prosperity to their God, since they were one of the smallest and most insignificant nations of that time. Consequently the other nations would proclaim that the God of Israel was truly God and that they would abandon their false gods and serve the Lord.

When Christ the Messiah came He revealed God's ultimate plan of salvation, He told His disciples to spread the truth (gospel) throughout the world. No longer was the truth hidden from the nations but it has been published throughout the earth. Therefore if people (nations) seek for the truth, it will be found. The truth of the gospel is that God has prepared a remedy for our sins; He has sent His Son Jesus Christ to satisfy the requirements of the law. Everyone who wishes to experience God's gift can now do so through faith in His Son. Once you have walked in the light of the truth, Satan is powerless to deceive you anymore regarding the plan of salvation. God never intended that Israel would have exclusive rights to Him but that the world through them would come to know Him. What Israel could not do because of their disobedience, God has accomplished in them through His Son. I will deal with the meaning of the 1000 years when we look at the saints reigning.

Chapter 10

Saints Reign a 1,000 Years
(Revelation 20:4-6)

And I saw thrones, and they sat upon them, and judgment was given unto them: and *I saw* the souls of them that were beheaded for the witness of Jesus, and for the word of God, and which had not worshipped the beast, neither his image, neither had received *his* mark upon their foreheads, or in their hands; and they lived and reigned with Christ a thousand years.

But the rest of the dead lived not again until the thousand years were finished. This *is* the first resurrection.

Blessed and holy *is* he that hath part in the first resurrection: on such the second death hath no power, but they shall be priests of God and of Christ, and shall reign with him a thousand years.

Revelation 20:4-6

L et's talk about this 1000 year timeframe, it doesn't seem to match any of the others numbers that we've dealt with so far. Here again we need to understand the Bibles use of numbers 1000 = 10 * 10 * 10 or 10 to the 3rd power. Ten is the number for human government[18]. The government sets the authoritative direction and moral conduct of man. We see this number used when God gives Israel the 10 commandments; these are laws by which they must govern themselves. Three is the number of the Holy Spirit or the complete Godhead (i.e. Father, Son and Holy Spirit).

What we have here is God creating His own kingdom on earth and establishing governmental rule through His Spirit. So 10 (human government) to the 3rd power (Godhead) = 1000 (Kingdom of God).

These facts lead us naturally to two questions.

1. When does the 1000 years begin?
2. When does the 1000 years end?

The 1000 years began at Pentecost (the birth of the church) and the 1000-year period will end with the rapture of the church.

Where does the part about the saints reigning come in? The saint's reign is the authority of the church through Jesus Christ; to reign means to have power over something or to prevail. The church is the body of Christ, that being the case it shares full authority with Him.

> *Mark 13:33 Take ye heed, watch and pray: for ye know not when the time is.*
> *Mark 13:34 For the **Son of man** is as a man taking a far journey, who left his house, and **gave authority to his servants**, and to every man his work, and commanded the porter to watch.*

From this parable we can see that the church has been given the full authority of Christ, in order to fulfill its ministry. Not only do we reign with Him but also we are ambassadors or representatives for Him on the earth.

> *2 Corinthians 5:20 Now then **we are ambassadors for Christ**, as though God did beseech [you] by us: we pray [you] in Christ's stead, be ye reconciled to God.*

The power, authority and responsibilities of the saints are awesome. But why don't we look like we're reigning? Where are the miracles and where is the manifestation of power? Christ has given His great authority to the Church but it's up to us (the church) to utilize it. We have to believe that we have the authority of Christ and our every action should be a demonstration of that fact.

Though Satan is bound (constrained by our legal authority) he is still busy deceiving many by obscuring the truth and filling the hearts of men with unbelief. Where there is unbelief there is a lessening of the power (reign) of God in the earth. Unfortunately this unbelief has even spread into the church itself, so the reign of God through the saints has been greatly diminished. Although the church has the legal authority over Satan, if it

45

fails to exercise those rights, its authority or reign becomes ineffective. Therefore it is imperative that we overcome the enemy through the weapons that Christ has provided for us.

1. **Believe** - to be covered by the blood of Christ (Salvation).
2. **Confess** - speak the Word of God over every circumstance (our testimony).

Satan is a defeated foe and he has but a short season left. So he is trying everything to prevent us from seeing the truth (Word of God). We have great liberty, power and authority in Christ but unfortunately Satan has even been able to dilute our faith. The Church must rise up and use the authority that it has in the earth through our Lord and Savior.

The last part of this vision talks about the 1st resurrection; it is broken into two groups. First those who came to life and reigned with Christ for a 1000 years and secondly those who will come to life after the 1000 years have expired. The first group is with Christ in heaven during the 1000-year period, they are the 144,000 of Israel (first fruits of God). Those that come to life afterwards are the great multitude described in Revelation chapter 7. Together both of these groups make up the 1st resurrection or the full harvest. The full harvest is synonymous with the term rapture. Everyone in these 2 groups is exempt from the second death, which is permanent separation from God that is symbolically shown as the lake of fire.

Chapter 11

The Revelation of Christ
(Revelation 1:9-20)

And in the midst of the seven candlesticks *one* like unto the Son of man, clothed with a garment down to the foot, and girt about the paps with a golden girdle.

His head and *his* hairs *were* white like wool, as white as snow; and his eyes *were* as a flame of fire;

And his feet like unto fine brass, as if they burned in a furnace; and his voice as the sound of many waters.

And he had in his right hand seven stars: and out of his mouth went a sharp twoedged sword: and his countenance *was* as the sun shineth in his strength.

Revelation 1:13-16

The description of Christ is given in the first chapter of Revelation but since this book is arranged by dispensation it naturally goes here before the letters to the 7 churches. This portrait of Christ is painted specifically for the 7 churches so that they will understand His role and relationship to it.

John goes through great pains to describe Christ but what is the purpose of such an enumerated description. Each element speaks of His character or nature. His clothing speaks of His office; a long garment (to the foot) and girdle are items of a King or High priest. Paul tells us in Hebrews that Christ has become our eternal high priest[19], reconciling us to God. His head and hair being white like wool denotes both His purity and wisdom. The head is the covering for the brain (mind), which controls the thoughts and actions of an individual. White is the symbol of purity and here it speaks to the purity of Christ thoughts and deeds. When white is used to reference the color of the hair, it expresses the wisdom of the aged. Christ is the ancient of days and is full of wisdom; therefore His every word and action display the great perspicacity of His personage.

His eyes like a flame of fire speak of His seeing past our actions right to our very motives. For God sees the heart and every intention of men. His feet like brass burned in the furnace shows us that he has been fully tried and tested by God. This points to His 1st advent as the Son of man He was tempted yet He was found blameless, righteous and holy. The Lord's voice was as the sound of many waters, here we see Christ speaking through many people. Many waters or seas represent nations/peoples; through the gentiles the church is a many nation entity symbolic for the body of Christ. John is showing us that God is Lord over all of creation; His voice speaks to and through every nation.

In His right hand are seven stars, this shows His special protection and care of the churches leaders for they must guide His flock. Out of his mouth went a two edged sword, this symbolizes the righteous judgment of the Lord (the Word of God). This sword is to kill the flesh (self-centeredness), so that we may live by the spirit (God-centered). Lastly His countenance like the sun speaks to His righteousness and His glory. The glory (appearance) of Christ is the same as God's; this speaks to the deity of Jesus as the Son of God.

The Lord Himself gave us the interpretation, the seven stars are seven angels over the churches and the seven golden lampstands are the seven churches themselves. The angels mentioned here are not literal angels, but they are the leaders or pastors of these churches. How do we know this because John is instructed to write to the 7 angels? Angels are messengers of God to mankind and not the contrary. Christ is seen in the middle or midst of the candlesticks (churches), meaning He is intimately acquainted with them and that He is constantly watching over them.

This vision of Christ shows us that He is undeniably worthy to judge the church and that His judgments are just and true. He has given His very life for the church and He has been given the responsibility of judging it. Judgment in this case is not a condemnation or punishment but it's a measuring stick or evaluation by the Word of God. It is a corrective step to insure that the children of God do not miss out on the fullness (best of) of the Lord's blessings.

Chapter 12

The 7 Letters
(Revelation 2 & 3)

The individual messages to the churches are pretty straightforward. It is significant to note that although a message is addressed to a specific church, each church was directed to read all 7 letters. Why? Because whatever the current state of the church was, it could easily fall into one of the other categories. Church leaders and lay people should evaluate each message to see what state their church is currently in, so that they can pray accordingly.

Remember that seven is God's number for completeness or perfection. So this message is to the Church as the whole and not just the seven indicated by name. Not only are these a letters for the Churches in John's time and locale but they are relevant to the church today.

There are three things that are being stressed to the Churches in these letters. We know that because they are repeated in each message to the churches.

1. I know your works...
2. He who has an ear...
3. He who overcomes...

First, "I know your works" whatever they are sometimes good, sometimes bad. The point is the Lord is well acquainted with our actions and us. There is no fooling God, remember He is the one who walks in the midst of the lampstands (churches).

The church needs to take an honest look at itself and follow the reproofs of our Lord, wherever it falls short. A business has quarterly reports, yearly reviews and long-range goals to measure it, so that it will stay on track. How much more does the church need to continually measure itself to stay on course? If a business fails all parties involved can always start over. If the church fails there is no starting over.

Secondly, "He who has an ear let him hear what the Spirit says to the churches". Put another way, whoever is wise or spiritual let him listen.

Why, because to them that are faithful there is encouragement. To them that are not, there is warning or correction. In either case it is imperative to hear the Spirit. If the faithful don't heed, they may faint. If the unfaithful refuse to listen, they will certainly be punished.

Lastly to "He who overcomes", belongs a reward. To him that overcomes what or whom, what is this overcoming exactly? To overcome means to win the victory over something. The world apart from God is condemned already because of sin. We must overcome or transcend this world in order to escape its condemnation.

As I stated earlier we overcome by the blood of the Lamb and the Word of God (testimony). But what's also involved is a daily battle of wills; we must relinquish our affections and attachments to this world. That can only happen by giving our total attention to pursing the will of God, to the point that we can say not my will but your will be done Lord. When we have reached this level in our daily lives then we have truly transcended or overcome the world.

It is especially sobering to note that only 2 out of the 7 churches are found blameless (without rebuke) that's less than 30 percent. There are of course individuals that are blameless within each church, but as a whole not even half of the church is found in right standing before God. This brings to mind the words of Jesus in the book of Matthew.

> *Matthew 7:21 ¶ Not every one that saith unto me, Lord, Lord, shall enter into the kingdom of heaven; but he that doeth the will of my Father which is in heaven.*
>
> *Matthew 7:22* **Many will say to me in that day, Lord, Lord, have we not prophesied in thy name? and in thy name have cast out devils? and in thy name done many wonderful works?**
>
> *Matthew 7:23 And then will* **I profess unto them, I never knew you: depart from me, ye that work iniquity.**

If we use the percentage we came up with 30% (rounded up), statistically speaking on average only 3 out of every 10 people in your congregation will actually enter the kingdom of heaven. Normally when reading Revelation we bypass the 7 letters in order to get to the meat of the book. Failing to recognize that we have been skipping the one of the most important parts. We need more than ever to hear what the Spirit is saying to the church (His people) today.

> **Note: The messages in these letters should be applied not only to churches but also to every individual.**

Message to Ephesus - 1ˢᵗ Church

> **"Unto the angel of the church of Ephesus write...Nevertheless I have somewhat against thee, because thou hast left thy first love. Remember therefore from whence thou art fallen, and repent, and do the first works; or else I will come unto thee quickly, and will remove thy candlestick out of his place, except thou repent."**

> ***Revelation 2:1-5***

In marriage you pledge your love forever to your spouse but when the stresses of everyday life come knocking repeatedly and newness of the relationship starts to fade. Combine to that the pressures of raising and providing for a family. When the responsibilities start to mount it becomes easy to see how we can lose track of the real reason we got married in the first place.

This is undoubtedly what happened to the church at Ephesus, they became so wrapped up in the other necessary things of the church that they gradually moved away from their first love. There were no outward signs of apostasy, false prophets or twisted doctrine. On the outside everything appeared to be just fine but inside their priorities were slowly shifting.

A couple doesn't ordinarily realize that they have failed to focus on each other until they are forced to be alone. Usually after the children leave home and that could be fatal to the marriage because too many years have slipped away.

Love must be constantly renewed, reaffirmed and refreshed to stay alive and vital. What is true of marriage is true of our walk with God. We must constantly be on guard against stagnation in our relationship with the Lord.

We expect God to always listen to us our prayers, complaints and desires. But is it a balanced relationship that we have with Him? If we don't spend time alone with God and listen to what's on His heart. How can we stay in His perfect will and how can we really please Him? If we don't make time alone with God a priority, we will find ourselves in the same predicament as the church in Ephesus.

If you find yourself lacking when you evaluate your relationship with the Lord all is not lost, simply admit your shortcomings and renew your relationship with Him now.

Message to Smyrna - 2nd Church

> **"I know thy works, and tribulation, and poverty, (but thou art rich)...Fear none of those things which thou shalt suffer: behold, the devil shall cast some of you into prison, that ye may be tried; and ye shall have tribulation ten days: be thou faithful unto death, and I will give thee a crown of life."**

Revelation 2:9,10

Would you join this church? I don't think I would, not with that description but yet this is a church that pleases God. The church of Smyrna is filled with tribulation (trouble) and poverty. As if that wasn't enough then the Lord states that more suffering is coming, but remain faithful till death.

What a contrast to today's Christian mentality, if we received that kind of prophecy today how many would remain in the church. Better yet how many would receive it as a word from the Lord. If the message is not blessings and prosperity many of us are not willing to listen.

Suffering, struggling, persecution and tribulations are no longer in the Christian's vocabulary. We have been misled to believe that through faith we do not have to suffer or struggle. While it is true that faith can move mountains, it is not always instantaneous.

As a child God told Joseph in a dream that he would rise above his family and that they would submit to him. He believed this but before this prophecy could be realized he was sold into slavery due to sibling jealously, he was later thrown in jail after being falsely accused by his master's wife. Joseph was well into his adulthood by the time that his faith materialized. What would happen to our belief system if we had to wait that long to receive our blessings.

We need to take the time to examine your motives for following Christ, are we following Him for the temporal blessings or for the eternal ones. If you focus mainly on the here and now, at some point your faith will suffer greatly. We must remember that the blessings we experience now are only a taste of what's ahead in the kingdom of God. So our primary goal should be on attaining the full blessing of the Lord in the eternal life, not in this one.

Message to Pergamos - 3rd Church

And to the angel of the church in Pergamos write; These things saith he which hath the sharp sword with two edges;

Revelation 2:12

The sword is a tool used for separation; here the Lord is calling out His people from those who hold questionable doctrine. What happens when you wash white clothes with colored ones? From experience we know that the colors will run and the whites will be ruined. Notice the white clothes don't run or ruin the colors it only works one way. The same holds true with believers and unbelievers, that mixing may cause ruin to the Christian's character but not the sinner's.

The church of Pergamos is commendable with the exception that some in the church, are following the teaching of Balaam and others the Nicolaitians. The problem is, if this situation is allowed to continue how long will the church's doctrine remain pure.

Ecclesia is the Greek word for church, meaning "called out ones". The apostle Paul states in the book of Romans, *Mark them which cause divisions and offences contrary to the doctrine which ye have learned; and avoid them*[20]. This does not mean we don't speak to those who don't believe or believe differently than we do. It simply means that we should be on guard against our faith becoming muddled. There is a saying, "evil company corrupts good manners".

It is unacceptable and almost unthinkable that the church would reject some people based on their personal belief system but that's what Paul admonished the church at Rome to do. Today it is politically incorrect to exclude anyone from participating in our church services. Anyone can walk into a church and take communion but that's not scriptural. Only believers are to take part in the actual act of communion.

Where do you stand on the issue of separation, do you tolerate what God considers wrong? I'm not talking about separating from people but practices like stealing, adultery, pornography, homosexuality, etc. Maybe those are too obvious how about things like little white lies, cheating on your taxes, showing favoritism. The Lord is calling His church to be a holy and peculiar people, to paraphrase it the Lord is summoning us to be a cut above the rest.

Message to Thyatira - 4ᵗʰ Church

I know thy works, and charity, and service, and faith, and thy patience, and thy works; and the last *to be* more than the first.
Notwithstanding I have a few things against thee, because thou sufferest that woman Jezebel, which calleth herself a prophetess, to teach and to seduce my servants to commit fornication, and to eat things sacrificed unto idols.

Revelation 2:19,20

Here we have a very commendable church but for one major exception, a false prophet or in this case a prophetess has slipped in and is beginning to lead the church astray. What does a false prophet look like? They will probably seem very pious. What does a false prophet sound like? They most likely will sound righteous. Then how do we guard against being misled in our spiritual walk?

*1 John 4:1 ¶ Beloved, **believe not every spirit, but try the spirits whether they are of God**: because many false prophets are gone out into the world.*
*1 John 4:2 **Hereby know ye the Spirit of God: Every spirit that confesseth that Jesus Christ is come in the flesh is of God**:*
1 John 4:3 And every spirit that confesseth not that Jesus Christ is come in the flesh is not of God: and this is that spirit of antichrist, whereof ye have heard that it should come; and even now already is it in the world.

I've highlighted part of this verse because so many today misquote it by saying, "Try the spirits, by the Spirit". This in itself will leave the door wide open to all sorts of false doctrine. John is exhorting us to test all doctrine by the infallible Word of God. If the teachings don't line up with the Bible, then don't accept them. That's simply enough to do, so why is it that we have so many contrary doctrines today?

*Acts 17:11   These were more noble than those in Thessalonica, in that they received the word with all readiness of mind, and **searched the scriptures daily, whether those things were so**.*

The fact is most Christians don't study the Bible regularly on their own. To become knowledgeable about the Bible you must study and studying is work. Regardless of the reasons behind why we don't study, this failure allows many false teachers to influence the church. The Word of God is often compared to being our food source (daily bread). If the only time we ingest the Word is on Sunday, then we are spiritually starving ourselves. In the natural if you starve yourself for a short period of time, you will eat almost anything because you're famished. So it is in the spiritual sense if you are not continuously feeding on the Word, you will be prone to deception (filling up on junk). In general a person who eats regularly, is far more discriminating in his or her food choices than someone that is famished.

Another prevalent problem today is that everyone, Christians included want to hear something that makes them feel good. We may hear something that sounds right or feels right but if it doesn't line up with the Word of God it's wrong. We become easy prey to seducing spirits, when we look for positive prophecies to prop up our egos. Many today use the ministry as if they were calling into the psychic hotline. We have become lazy; we don't want to deal with our problems by utilizing faith and standing on the Word of God. Most Christians are looking for someone to tell them what their next move should be, that is religious witchcraft plain and simple.

A quick survey through the Old Testament and we will see that prophecies to individuals were few and far in between. Not only that but most times it was years before the prophecy was fulfilled and if they received another prophecy in the meantime it was usually an affirmation of the first one. Today it's not unusual for people to have 4 and 5 different prophecies a year. And God forbid someone receives a really good one and the minister passes over us, we feel slighted. We think why didn't God say anything to me, is there something wrong in my life, because I really need to hear from God too.

We do not need someone telling us they see blessing in our lives, God's word already declares that. If God said it, why do we constantly look to man for confirmation? People run from church to church and minister-to-minister to find out what they should be doing. God is not in the fortune telling business, He has given us the liberty to make our own choices in life.

Admittedly some have a special call on their lives and if your one of those people trust me, God knows how to communicate that to you. Most of us however are free to choose our own vocations, mates, etc. without a prophetic word from on high. The only prerequisite is that we prayerfully make our choices; God's word assures us that He will direct us by His Spirit.

If we will take time everyday to pray and study the Word, we will eliminate the possibility of being led astray by false doctrine.

Message to Sardis - 5ᵗʰ Church

> **And unto the angel of the church in Sardis write; These things saith he that hath the seven Spirits of God, and the seven stars; I know thy works, that thou hast a name that thou livest, and art dead.**
> **Be watchful, and strengthen the things which remain, that are ready to die: for I have not found thy works perfect before God.**

> *Revelation 3:1,2*

The church of Sardis has one of the best reputations of all the churches, if any church of the 7 churches was really alive this was the one. But wait God declares that this church is dead! Something is really wrong here and we need to see that clearly. Man's opinion including those in the body of Christ is not necessarily God's.

No one would want to go to a church that God considers dead, so how should we pick a place of worship? One criterion we might use is membership, if the congregation is large and growing, that's usually a good indicator. Having various ministries to meet the needs of the people, such as children's church, teen's ministry, young adults, couples fellowship, singles gathering etc is another sign. Let's not forget about the preacher, he or she should be dynamic, anointed and spiritually gifted. How about the fact that people come from every direction just to experience one of this church's services and every night the building is packed to capacity. Unfortunately none of these things can be used as a trustworthy gauge to see if this church is really alive in the sight of God. A church may have all of these qualities and still miss the mark.

Remember Smyrna the 2nd Church, God was well please with this group of believers. They suffered through various tribulations and were poor, most likely they were small in comparison to the church of Sardis. To top it all off, it was prophesied that they would have to endure even more persecution. Is there any wonder that the masses would flock to the church of Sardis over Smyrna? In fact the church in Smyrna doesn't seem to have any of the criteria to draw us into their membership.

Obviously what we need in this situation is the mind of the Lord. We cannot go by our own thoughts, feelings or instincts for only God can search the heart. Only through diligence in prayer, can we hope to gain the mind of the Lord. Although a church may be excelling others in growth, programs and ministries, that does not mean that the church as a whole is fulfilling the will of God. The church is called to be a witness and to reconcile mankind back to God. Too many programs and activities can cause the church to lose its primary focus - souls.

As a church begins to grow it's easy to lose track of its original purpose, there are so many needs to be met. There are legitimate obligations that the church must attend to; organizations are formed to meet the various needs. Every thing is growing, changing and shifting, multiple priorities confront the ministry. Therefore it is critical that the church takes time to sit quietly before God, and allow Him to set the agenda. Otherwise we labor in vain and our work is not pleasing to the Lord. Although we may have the best of intentions, busily doing exemplary things, we could wind up falling short of the mark.

Take time and assess the areas your church spends the majority of its time and resources? The members are the church, so whatever activity the church is focusing on that's what the members are concentrating on. To put it plainly, where the head goes the body follows. Since our very souls are at stake here, we need to be absolutely certain that our church is working on God's true priorities.

Message to Philadelphia - 6th Church

> **Because thou hast kept the word of my patience, I also will keep thee from the hour of temptation, which shall come upon all the world, to try them that dwell upon the earth.**

> *Revelation 3:10*

Sadly, Philadelphia is only the second church that does not receive a rebuke.

The key to this and every church's success is patience; being steadfast despite opposition, difficulty or adversity. The church of Philadelphia evidently has persevered through opposition and for that God will reward them. He has promised to keep them from the hour of temptation, which will come upon the world. This hour of temptation is not the same as the great tribulation but rather it's the day of wrath.

Lets first look at the wording, hour of temptation and what exactly is this temptation? The <u>hour</u> of temptation is a contrast to the <u>day</u> of tribulation; the emphasis is on the duration or time frame of the event. The word temptation would be better rendered trial or affliction.

> *Deuteronomy 4:33 Did ever people hear the voice of God speaking out of the midst of the fire, as thou hast heard, and live?*
> *Deuteronomy 4:34 Or hath God assayed to go and take him a nation from the midst of another nation, **by temptations**, by signs, and by wonders, and by war, and by a mighty hand, and by a stretched out arm, and by great terrors, according to all that the LORD your God did for you in Egypt before your eyes?*

Israel was brought out of Egypt by the awesome trials or afflictions (temptations) God placed upon the nation. So the hour of temptation should be interpreted as the hour of affliction. Exemption from the coming wrath is the reward of the church of Philadelphia and also to present day believers for enduring the great tribulation. As we discussed earlier in the book Christians suffer through tribulation, due to the great wrath of Satan. But God is not allowing His people to arbitrarily suffer; tribulation has a place in our lives.

> *Romans 5:3   And not only so, but we glory in tribulations also: knowing that **tribulation worketh patience;***

We are told in St. Luke that "...in patience posses ye your souls"[21]. Whenever you have done all to stand, you need patience to remain steadfast in your faith. Without it we would faint, we would grow weary in doing the Lord's will. If we fail to hold out till the end, the loss would be monumental. Paul puts it this way, "For I reckon that the sufferings of this present time are not worthy to be compared with the glory which shall be revealed in us"[22].

Our rewards, achievements or successes that we receive here on earth will pale in comparison to what awaits us in glory. But only he or she who overcomes will receive their reward. We must therefore watch and pray, giving due diligence to our faith. The voice of the Lord is calling out to His people today saying, "Behold, I come quickly; and my reward is with me, to give every man according as his work shall be"[23].

Message to Laodicea - 7th Church

I know thy works, that thou art neither cold nor hot: I would thou wert cold or hot. So then because thou art lukewarm, and neither cold nor hot, I will spue thee out of my mouth.

Revelation 3:15,1

Through the church of Philadelphia we heard the Lord calling us to a state of readiness, here we get a foretaste of what will happen if we are not. This church is rich and self-satisfied, they obviously believe that they are doing right. Yet these Christians leave such a lukewarm taste in the Lord's mouth, they are about to be spit out. This is by far the sternest rebuke from Jesus, so we definitely need to see the reasons behind it.

To be a lukewarm Christian is to be without conviction or to be halfhearted in your commitment to Christ. That brings us to our next question what does Jesus require of us? *"If any man will come after me, let him deny himself, and take up his cross daily, and follow me."*[24] The answer is threefold self-denial, daily crucifying the flesh and following Christ via the Spirit.

Self-denial in relation to Jesus means to forgo your own desires (even if they're good), in order to fulfill God's holy will. Denial is not pleasant or easy when done out of duty but this is meant to be a response of love. Crucifying the flesh daily (taking up the cross) means to count yourself as dead to sin, in order to live in Christ (righteousness). This can only be done by faith; we need to daily affirm through the Word that sin has no more dominion over us. Declaring our flesh to be dead, that we my live through the Spirit.

> **Without confessing and believing the Word (faith) on this matter true victory cannot be won.**

Lastly, following the Spirit (Jesus) is being obedient to His Word and what His Spirit would speak to your heart. If ever there is a conflict between what you believe the Spirit is saying and the Word of God, obey the Word. Obedience to the Word implies knowledge of God's Word and that only comes through careful study.

If you claim to be a believer and you are not actively denying yourself, crucifying the flesh and following God's Word (Christ). You run the risk of being a lukewarm Christian and are in danger of being spit out of the mouth of God. We can never become satisfied in our walk but we must always strive have more of Christ in our lives. Sadly, I believe many today fall into same category as this church. **God is calling us to be fervent and dedicated in our commitment to the Lord, hear what the Spirit is saying to your heart today.**

Chapter 13

The 7 Trumpets
(Revelation 8:6-9:21)

T he seven trumpets of God are now ready to be blown, actually this event and everything else that we've described so far in this section start in the same general time period. Trumpets were used in the Old Testament to sound a warning or to gather the people together for an assembly. Their purpose is the same here these trumpets are to place us in a state of readiness (alert), we will examine the first six trumpets (warnings) in this chapter and the 7th one we'll address in the next section (the Future).

1ˢᵗ Trumpet

> **The first angel sounded, and there followed hail and fire mingled with blood, and they were cast upon the earth: and the third part of trees was burnt up, and all green grass was burnt up.**

> *Revelation 8:7*

What John is seeing here does not happen all at once. If one third of our forests were destroyed at one time, it would throw the earth's ecology out of control. This first trumpet started hundreds of years ago and will continue until we have reached one third. This occurrence of course is not to be taken literally by John; this symbolism is only to tell us that the trees and grass will be destroyed.

We don't have to look far to see the fulfillment of this trumpet; the newspapers are filled with articles about the devastation and destruction of our forests and lands. Fires burn out of control every year, leaving millions in damage. Man himself is probably the biggest culprit with an unsatiable appetite for wood products, fueling logging efforts. Chemical fallout from accidents and illegal dumping also rob us of our precious land. These are just a few of the ways this trumpet is being fulfilled before our eyes. Look around today and see what percentage of our lands has been rendered unusable?

A quick look at the forest excluding other plant life tells us that approximately 47% of our forest original forest cover is left. The Food and Agriculture Organization estimates for 1900-95 we were losing 112,600 square kilometers per year (approx. 33 soccer fields per minute).[25] We have not only reached the one-third mark but we have surpassed it, the first trumpet has definitely sounded.

2nd Trumpet

> **And the second angel sounded, and as it were a great mountain burning with fire was cast into the sea: and the third part of the sea became blood;**
> **And the third part of the creatures which were in the sea, and had life, died; and the third part of the ships were destroyed.**

> *Revelation 8:8,9*

Here we have a picture of one third of all sea life dying and also a third of the sea vessels being destroyed. Again this does not happen all at once but it is a gradual occurrence. The sea becoming blood would be a poisoning or rendering the waters unlivable for sea life. A probable means of such destruction would be pollution from legal and illegal dumping. Some examples would be seepage from landfills, sewage treatment plants, oils, bacterial waste, nuclear waste and pesticides contained in storm water runoff from paved surfaces.

The American Fisheries Society has published its first ever list of marine fish stocks at risk of extinction in North America. The AFS had a similar list for freshwater fish 20 years ago, but only recently have they recognized that marine species are also vulnerable to extinction. The list includes 82 species and subspecies listed as endangered in North America with 22 species categorized as endangered with global extinction. The population status and life histories of many marine species is inadequate at this time, so this should be regarded as a starting point rather that the final version.[26] Therefore it is impossible to get a definitive percentage of sea life that has been destroyed but the number is probably already over the 1/3 mark.

One side effect from poisoning the waters is that we indirectly contaminate our food chain. By polluting the waters we poison the sea life, we in turn introduce harmful carcinogens into our bodies by consuming fish and other seafood's. Even our recreational time suffers; water that is too harmful for fishing is also unhealthy for swimming and other water sports.

The reference to ships being destroyed implies wars, crashes and storms this would include all boats, ships, submarines or any other sea vessel. Again it is very easy to see the fulfillment of this trumpet. Normally we look for great ominous signs from God but most of the events in Revelation are manifested through what we consider natural occurrences.

3rd Trumpet

And the third angel sounded, and there fell a great star from heaven, burning as it were a lamp, and it fell upon the third part of the rivers, and upon the fountains of waters;

And the name of the star is called Wormwood: and the third part of the waters became wormwood; and many men died of the waters, because they were made bitter.

Revelation 8:10,11

The second trumpet affected the sea life; this trumpet directly impacts man's drinking water. The source of this contamination is not a literal star from heaven but sadly it's man himself, who is cutting off his own vital supply. A third of our water supply will become undrinkable; the causes would be the same as those listed in the second trumpet.

The importance of water to us cannot be over emphasized; it is to our bodies a miracle fluid. Its chemical and physical properties are especially suited to be the perfect solvent in the human body[27]. In order for the body to perform properly we need optimum water saturation of cells and tissues. Contamination of this essential resource will naturally destroy the organism (our bodies) itself.

In a recent report by the U.S. PIRG (Public Interest Research Group) nearly 30% of the nation's largest industrial, municipal and federal facilities were in serious violation of the Clean Water Act at least once during a 15-month period. At the same time 40% of the nation's waterways are considered too polluted for safe fishing or swimming. The EPA identified more than 600 chemicals that are hazardous to human health or the environment. Nearly 270 million pounds of toxic chemicals were released into American waterways in one year, either directly or through water treatment facilities. Almost 11 million pounds of these chemicals are either cancer causing, persistent in the environment or cause reproductive problems in humans.[28]

When I was growing up in the United States it was unheard of to buy drinking water. After all why would someone buy water, when you could get all you wanted for free? Now water can cost more than soft drinks and no one wants to drink from the tap anymore. Look how rapidly our water sources are being depleted; do you hear the sound of 3rd trumpet?

4th Trumpet

And the fourth angel sounded, and the third part of the sun was smitten, and the third part of the moon, and the third part of the stars; so as the third part of them was darkened, and the day shone not for a third part of it, and the night likewise.

Revelation 8:12

Because of the usage of the sun, moon and the stars, this passage becomes a little unclear. Previously (in the 6th seal) this was the Father, Son and His angels? We can take two approaches to interpret this particular passage, either physical or spiritual. Four is the number for creation and this is the 4th trumpet. If we look at the first four seals, trumpets and bowls we will see that they all deal directly with creation. I'm going to choose the physical interpretation here. If the fourth trumpet were not physical then it would break the pattern, which is my reasoning for going with this method of interpretation.

"Since I believe that this sign is physical then what we have occurring here is a darkening or dimming of the natural light sources for a third of the world. How can that be, what would cause only a third of the planet to be dimmed? The phenomenon is called regional hazing. Virtually all of our national parks and wilderness areas are subject to some degree of regional haze visibility impairment. This fact has been well documented by the National Park Service, EPA, the United States Forest Service, and other agencies since 1978. Haze obscures the clarity, color, texture, and form of what we see. It is caused by natural and anthropogenic pollutants that are emitted to the atmosphere through a number of activities, such as electric power generation, various industrial and manufacturing processes, car and truck emissions, burning activities, and so on. These emissions often are transported long distances to the Class I areas identified for protection under the Clean Air Act."

"We also know that the causes and severity of regional haze vary greatly between the East and the West. The average visual range in most of the Western U.S. is 60 to 90 miles, or about one-half to two-thirds of the visual range that would exist without manmade air pollution. In most of the East, the average visual range is less than 18 miles, or about one-fifth of the visual range that would exist under natural conditions. One of the major challenges associated with this problem is that these conditions are often caused not by one single source near each park or wilderness area, but by mixing of emissions from a wide variety of sources over a broad region."[29] Here again we can see the clear fulfillment of another trumpet.

5th Trumpet and 1st Woe

> **And the fifth angel sounded, and I saw a star fall from heaven unto the earth: and to him was given the key of the bottomless pit.**
>
> *Revelation 9:1*

What is this trumpet trying to describe? It sounds like a plague of some sort, but what type of plague will strike only those who do not have the seal of God. We already know that this seal is given to all of God's children; it is the seal of the Holy Spirit. If God's people were physically isolated somehow from the rest of the world, I could see this happening. But God's people are everywhere; dispersed throughout the earth. I have to be honest my head started hurting with this one; I just couldn't figure this out. I had to step back and pray again, because I knew the answer was right in front of me (in the scriptures). Here's the key "I saw a star fallen from heaven to the earth..."

> *St. Luke 10:17 ¶ And the seventy returned again with joy, saying, Lord, even the devils are subject unto us through thy name.*
> *St. Luke 10:18 And he said unto them, **I beheld Satan as lightning fall from heaven.***

> *St. Luke 10:19   Behold, I give unto you power to tread on **serpents and scorpions, and over all the power of the enemy**: and nothing shall by any means hurt you.*
> *St. Luke 10:20   Notwithstanding in this rejoice not, that the spirits are subject unto you; but rather rejoice, because your names are written in heaven.*

Satan is that star (angel) fallen from heaven.   The fact that the sun and the air are darkened points to the devices that he uses to obscure the true light (Word of God).   As for the plague, well there is no plague.   This is where my thinking went askew.   Satan (the enemy) does not have the authority to harm God's people, but all others are within his dominion.

What once so bewildered me now seems so clear.   The reference to scorpions and locusts and their king Apollyon or Abaddon really had me thinking.   These names translated mean Destroyer and Destruction; the destroyer is another name for Satan.   By reading the passage in Luke, we can plainly see that serpents and scorpions are references to devils or demons.   But when I looked in Revelation and saw scorpions and locusts I got lost in the imagery.   Thank God He has left keys and clues all over His Word for all who seek His wisdom.

The sting of Satan or rather his demons is their ability to induce sin in the lives of people.   The Christian is exempt from this but only when they are actively following the Spirit of God.   For the bible clearly states that all who "walk in the Spirit, will not obey the lust of the flesh"[30].   As for the unbelievers and those Christians who do not walk after the Spirit, they will suffer the various consequences of their sins.

The 5th Trumpet is actually a more detailed look into John's vision in Revelation chapter 12 concerning the "War on Earth".   Satan has fallen to the earth (1st Woe) after Christ has risen victoriously from the grave.   He has the power to strike or afflict man but not to kill him.   The devil's authority over man is for 5 months; this represents incompleteness as we saw earlier with the 5 seals.   Satan's power over man is only partial, because man has the ability to break the devil's dominion over his life through Christ Jesus.

This is the 1st of 3 woes given to the inhabitants of the earth.   The fifth, sixth and seventh trumpets will cause much misery (woes) to mankind.   We need to pay special attention to these trumpets because of the grief that is associated to them.   Remember that the trumpets are warnings, so there is a way to avoid the misery that these trumpets bring and Jesus Christ is that way.

6th Trumpet and 2nd Woe

6th Trumpet and 2nd Woe

> **And thus I saw the horses in the vision, and them that sat on them, having breastplates of fire, and of jacinth, and brimstone: and the heads of the horses *were* as the heads of lions; and out of their mouths issued fire and smoke and brimstone.**
>
> **By these three was the third part of men killed, by the fire, and by the smoke, and by the brimstone, which issued out of their mouths.**

Revelation 9:17,18

Without the full understanding of the 5th trumpet, we cannot grasp the meaning of this vision because the two are linked together. This trumpet is also a more detailed look into Revelation chapter 12, the "War on Earth". In the previous trumpet Satan after being hurled to earth was enticing mankind to sin and consequently to suffer the ramifications of our fleshly actions. This time Satan and his horde are going to war against man, for the possession of his soul (2nd Woe).

The colors of the horsemen's breastplates correspond to the plagues that come out of the horses' mouths. The color red or fire speaks of death; remember the red horse in the 2nd seal? Blue (jacinth) or smoke represents deception, a obscuring of the truth. Lastly, Yellow or brimstone expresses the idea of excruciating pain, a type of pestilence.

The Christian has no exemption from this trumpet, as he did from the previous one. That is because Christians are the primary targets of this assault. Satan is sending deception, death and pestilence to nullify the effects of the gospel in our lives. This should not be news to believers; the adversary has been using these tactics from the beginning. Most Christians are familiar with the scripture that says, "the thief cometh not but to steal (deception) and to kill (death) and to destroy (pestilence)"[31]. I think when we hear the term thief; it conveys the wrong picture in our mind. Satan is not trying to pickpocket people but he desires to destroy us.

Don't be fooled this is an all out war; most believers don't act like their engaged in a battle. That's the beauty of it if you don't see this as a war, then you won't fight. Once you buy into that deception, you're no threat to the enemy. We think that we're just making a choice to serve God or not, but actually the decision is to fight or be killed. Many think that because they are good people or that they treat everyone fairly, that they are okay with God. It's not about how good your are or how moral you live, all that matters is what side you choose to be on.

At the end of this vision we see that 1/3 of mankind has been killed. Christians are definitely included in that number, we are susceptible to being killed either on purpose or by accident. If we don't continually watch and pray, we can be deceived. Even though God does provide healing, sicknesses can and does invade the believers' bodies. What then is the point of believing? We must keep in mind that the battle is not for our bodies but for our souls and our eternal destination. That's why the sting of death is sin, because sin (our sin nature) separates us from God. But Christ gives us the victory (through believing and confessing Him), by reconnecting us to the Father and giving us eternal life in Him.

When this vision ends mankind still does not repent of their sins. Why, because death (murders, suicides and wars), deception (false religions, cults, humanism) and pestilence (cancer, AIDS, viruses) will seem commonplace. All of this is meant to turn us back to God but instead man is turning to sociology, psychology and science for answers. There is a large gap between the 6th and the 7th trumpets. This delay allows the gospel to be preached throughout the world and gives mankind a space of time for repentance. How long is this time for repentance, that the church calls grace? God does not tell us, He simply admonishes us to be ready because when the 7th and final trumpet sounds it will be too late.

Chapter 14

The Beast out of the Sea
(Revelation 13:1-10)

And I stood upon the sand of the sea, and saw a beast rise up out of the sea, having seven heads and ten horns, and upon his horns ten crowns, and upon his heads the name of blasphemy.

And the beast which I saw was like unto a leopard, and his feet were as *the feet* of a bear, and his mouth as the mouth of a lion: and the dragon gave him his power, and his seat, and great authority.

Revelation 13:1,2

The beast out of the sea, here we come to one of the most misunderstood chapters in the whole bible. There are two beasts described in the 13th chapter of Revelation and their true identity has remained a subject of debate for quite sometime. I thought the fifth trumpet had my head spinning, compared to this chapter that was only the tip of the iceberg. Let's dive right in; we have a beast rising up out of the sea. This is significant because the other beast rises from the earth. So what is the importance or meaning of the sea?

*Revelation 17:15 And he saith unto me, The **waters** which thou sawest, where the whore sitteth, **are peoples, and multitudes, and nations, and tongues.***

Water or seas represent masses of people from many nations. This is alluded to in Revelation 13:7, but it is almost impossible to catch without the above verse. The beast has seven heads and ten horns, each horn has a crown and the dragon gave him his power, throne and authority. Well, we already know from Revelation 12 that the dragon represents Satan. So it's the devil that is giving his power, throne and authority to the beast. The world marvels and follows the beast, because it was fatally wounded but

Robert R. Davis

lived. The beast speaks blasphemous words against God. He is given authority and allowed to continue 42 months.

Forty-two months, didn't we see that number somewhere before? Yes we did, the 42 months is equivalent to 3 ½ years the church has to witness. So what we see here is another view of the same time period as the two witnesses prophecy and Israel's wilderness experience. The beast will make war with the saints and overcome (kill) them. Here is the patience of the saints, for they will be led captive and killed (physically) for the sake of Christ and the gospel.

This beast has 7 heads with 7 crowns; Revelation chapter 17 tells us that the heads represent kings (actually kingdoms). The crowns of course indicate rulership, so each kingdom actually rules supreme during their specific time period. We are also told that the 10 horns are ten kings that have not received a kingdom yet. Since the two beasts are so closely linked, if we can identify one that should reveal to us the other.

> *Revelation 17:9   And here is the mind which hath wisdom. **The seven heads are seven mountains**, on which the woman sitteth.*

"The city of seven hills is also called the eternal city, because it has been one of the world's great cities for more than 2,500 years. Over the years it has had it's periods of glory and decline. But it has always returned, as a center of art, learning, religion and government, that city can only be Rome"[32]. The beast that rises out of the sea represents the Roman Empire.

Now that we have identified the first beast, let's see how it fits the vision. The world worships the beast saying, "Who is like the beast (Rome)? Who is able to make war with him?" That was certainly the sentiment of the people during Rome's zenith. Rome was allowed to make war with the saints and to overcome them. It is a well-known fact that Rome persecuted and killed scores of Christians.

The dragon (Satan) gives his authority to the beast. Although Satan is at war with the saints (Revelation 12), notice how he uses Rome as his vehicle to perform his attacks. Authority was given to him (the beast) over every tribe, tongue, and nation. Rome ruled the western world and was arguably the greatest empire in the history of mankind. Rome demanded worship from its subjects, some emperors even declared themselves as gods. Anyone who opposed them was put to death, for defying the supreme power. Clearly Rome fits the description of the beast out of the sea.

Note: Rome is not the only beast for the beast has 7 heads and 10 horns, Rome is just one of the heads. The beast represents the world's system without God.

We will discuss this in more detail, when we review the 17th chapter of Revelation. The whole beast therefore represents the world's kingdoms or nations. It is interesting to note is how Satan can influence governments to do his bidding. We need to follow the apostle Paul's advice about praying for all people in authority (the government), because we never know who or what is influencing our decision-makers.

Chapter 15

The Beast out of the Earth
(Revelation 13:11-18)

> **And I beheld another beast coming up out of the earth; and he had two horns like a lamb, and he spake as a dragon.**
> **And he exerciseth all the power of the first beast before him, and causeth the earth and them which dwell therein to worship the first beast, whose deadly wound was healed.**
>
> *Revelation 13:11,12*

We have here another beast, this time coming from the earth. We should note that whatever the beast represents, it ascends from below the earth. Therefore it is not of God, for whatever is from God descends or come down from heaven. The beast has two horns like a lamb but speaks like a dragon. So its outward appearance is like that of Christ but it speaks as the devil speaks (deceitfully). It's the proverbial wolf in sheep's clothing.

This beast and the first beast exist together and they exercise equal authority. This 2nd beast causes people to worship the first one, with great signs and miracles occurring by its power.

> *Revelation 19:20 And the beast was taken, and with him* ***the false prophet that wrought miracles before him***, *with which he deceived them that had received the mark of the beast, and them that worshipped his image. These both were cast alive into a lake of fire burning with brimstone.*

In Revelation chapter 19 the second beast is also called the false prophet, this is consistent with his ability to perform signs and wonders. This prophet causes all people from every economic status to receive the mark of the first beast. This is not by force but through deception. Well, who is this beast or false prophet? The bible says, "here is wisdom, his number is 666.

We are told to calculate the number for it is the number of a man. But will this number give us the number of the first or second beast. If we look carefully we will see that this is the number of the first beast. Calculating the number 666 in Hebrew, Latin or any other language for that fact, will give you almost any name you associate with it. The common belief is that it stands for Caesar Nero; most scholars disagree with this due to the date difference between Nero's rule and John writing. If 666 points to Nero it is likely to be due to the fact that he more or less personified the evil of the Empire to those of the Christian faith at the time of John's writing. He slaughtered untold numbers of Christian's by wild animals before crowds of spectators in the arena, while others were tied to posts, covered with flammable material and used as human street lamps for his gardens. If we go with the common opinion pointing this number to Nero, this still links us to the 1st beast being Rome or the Roman Empire.

Also the worship of the beast or the false trinity (666) must be close in nature to the true worship of the heavenly trinity, otherwise how would people be deceived. I submit that this beast or false prophet is not a human since no person could live as long as the empire existed. What then does this beast represent?

> *Revelation 11:3 ¶ And I will give power unto my **two witnesses,** and they **shall prophesy** a thousand two hundred and threescore days, clothed in sackcloth.*

The two witnesses or prophets here represent the church as we have already established. The same rule should hold true here also or else it becomes almost impossible to interpret the scripture. So the second beast or false prophet is a church or religion, not an actual prophet. There are many false religions today, but the one represented here is directly linked to the first beast. We have already established that Rome or the Roman Empire is the first beast, logically then the second beast must be the Church of Rome and the Roman Catholic Church. The Church of Rome was succeeded or replaced by the Roman Catholic Church. But wait, before we accept this interpretation lets check it against the vision.

The Church of Rome was clearly pagan but does the Roman Catholic Church really fit the description of the second beast?

1. The second beast will have the same authority as the first.

"The Edict of Milan, a cluster of documents issued by Constantine the Great in 313 ad., made Christianity a lawful religion, by the end of the 4th century it had become the state religion. Historians call the church of this period the Constantine church, designating the privileged position of the church within the state…The privileged position appears to be the fact that **the church could contend with the state on equal terms and sometimes win the conflict**".[33]

2. The second beast will cause people to worship the 1st beast.

"Emperor worship was also encouraged officially, however, as a focus of common loyalty for the polyglot empire".[34] "For a time, **coins and other monuments continued to link Christian doctrines** with the worship of the sun, to which Constantine had been addicted previously. But even when this phase came to an end, Roman paganism continued to exert other, permanent influences, great and small. The emperors passed on to the popes the title of chief priest, pontifex maximus. The saints (sainthood), with their distribution of functions, often seemed to perpetuate the many numina (A presiding divinity) of ancient tradition."[35]

3. Performs great signs and wonders.

Even today we have statues that drip oil or bleed and various apparitions of the Virgin Mary throughout the world.

4. Gives breathe to the beast so that the image should speak.

"It appears that…Christianity would destroy the Roman Empire if it destroyed paganism. They were correct in their evaluation of the Christian ethos, but they did not foresee that Christianity would reach a compromise with the empire, that it would become 'Roman'."[36] Therefore instead of destroying the empire, it infused it with life and prolonged its existence.

5. <u>That it would cause as many that would not worship the beast to be killed</u>.

The inquisitions of the 13th century show the intolerance and treatment of those who did not agree with the church. This practice directly imitated emperor worship, for those who did not worship the emperor or his image suffered martyrdom.

I deliberately quoted from the encyclopaedia because I wanted a historical record, not a religiously biased opinion of the empire and the church. These facts should prove that the Church of Rome and the Roman Catholic Church are indeed the second beast, described by John. It is also interesting to note that even the New American Catholic Bible Personal Study Edition[37] points to Rome as the 1st beast, with Nero the most likely candidate to be equated to 666. If the 1st beast is the Roman Empire to whom else but the church could the 2nd beast be referring?

Remember that the beast as a whole represents the world's kingdoms, so the false prophet in its entirety would have to symbolize the world's religions or it's belief systems. I only identified the Church of Rome and the Roman Catholic Church, because it was specifically mentioned in connection with the Roman Empire. The empire typified the beast of the sea at the time of John's writing. The problem with the church (2nd Beast) lies not necessarily in the people but the dogma they follow. Remember the description of the 2nd beast he looks like a lamb but he speaks like a dragon. On the outside he looks Christ like but his words are deceptive.

We all need to know what we believe and more importantly, we know to see if our religious doctrine lines up with the Word of God.

I'm speaking of course to those of the Christian faith, regardless of your particular denomination. We must keep in mind that our religions are man made, that's why the 2nd beast rises from the earth. God has only ordained following the law (Judaism in its strictest sense) and the Spirit (Christianity in its purest form), every other religion comes from man and is prone to fallacies.

As far as the mark of the beast is concerned, I do not believe this to be a literal or physical mark. Why would God condemn anyone for an external symbol, Jesus taught us that its not what's on the outside but the inside that of man that condemns (defiles) us before God.[38]

Robert R. Davis

> *Revelation 14:1 And I looked, and, lo, a Lamb stood on the mount Sion, and with him **an hundred forty [and] four thousand, having his Father's name written in their foreheads.***

Just as God's people have his mark or seal, so it is with the beast and his people. The Lord certainly can tell those who are his and those who are not. Concerning the issue of people not being able to buy or sell without the mark or the image of the beast, this refers to the currency of that time.

> *Matthew 22:18 But Jesus perceived their wickedness, and said, Why tempt ye me, [ye] hypocrites?* •
> *Matthew 22:19 **Shew me the tribute money**. And they brought unto him a penny.*
> *Matthew 22:20 And he saith unto them, **Whose [is] this image and superscription?***
> *Matthew 22:21 They say unto him, **Caesar's**. Then saith he unto them, Render therefore unto Caesar the things which are Caesar's; and unto God the things that are God's.*

All of the coins had the images of either dead or living emperor's on one side and their accomplishments on the back. But we also see from Jesus' statement that the people were not condemned for using the money. The reference was only used to give us the identity of the first beast (Rome).

Let's take another tact at deciphering the number 666; six is God's number for man. So the 666 is man's number that has been formed into a trinity. So this number would indicate that man is exalting himself as God (this was a common practice of the emperor's of Rome). All who receive the mark of the beast shall be judged of the Lord. Remember the beast as a whole symbolizes the world's kingdoms or just the world. So receiving the mark of the beast means having the mark of the world. This makes sense because all that do not have the seal of God bear the mark of the world.

The seal denotes ownership specifically by royalty. When you apply the seal to people, it implies citizenship (kingdom of God). The mark also denotes ownership, but when applied to humans it implies slavery or bondage (literally property). We know that the seal of God is not a literal stamp, yet all Christians bear this seal. From this we then can deduce that the mark of the world is not a literal symbol either. The number of the mark is 666 (the number of man forming a unholy trinity); the number of the seal is then 333 (the number of the Spirit forming a holy trinity).

76

> **All who bear the mark cannot enter the kingdom of God, so the mark must be spiritual in nature not physical.**

Numbers are often used inconspicuously throughout the Bible, they are not always explicitly mentioned but sometimes we must count various descriptions to get their true meaning. For example in the following scripture we see that the church is to be a witness to the world, we are told this with words and numbers. Four is the number for creation or the world, so the church is told to witness to the entire world both implicitly and explicitly.

> *Acts 1:8 But ye shall receive power, after that the Holy Ghost is come upon you: and **ye shall be witnesses** unto me both in **Jerusalem**, and in all **Judaea**, and in **Samaria**, and unto the **uttermost part of the earth**.*

1. Jerusalem
2. Judaea
3. Samaria
4. Uttermost parts of the earth (world)

With this new knowledge in hand, what sign would distinguish a Christian from a non-Christian? Every believer is sealed with the Holy Spirit of promise. If we find all of the places that numbers or descriptions are used in connection to the Holy Spirit, we should find our answer. The seal of God is 333, which forms the Lord's holy trinity! We commonly call this the fruit of the Spirit.

> *Galatians 5:22 But the **fruit of the Spirit** is love, joy, peace, longsuffering, gentleness, goodness, faith,*
> *Galatians 5:23 Meekness, temperance: against such there is no law.*

| Love | Longsuffering | Faith |
| Joy | Gentleness | Meekness |
Peace	Goodness	Temperance
3	3	3

Clearly this is the seal or sign that every Christian must bear, to be allowed in the kingdom of God. Now it becomes fairly obvious what the mark of the world is. It's located in the same passage as the fruit of the Spirit; this is commonly called the works of the flesh.

Note: We are told to calculate the number the number of the beast. To identify this scripture we had to count or calculate the number of descriptions in this passage.

Galatians 5:19 **Now the works of the flesh are manifest,** *which are [these]; Adultery, fornication, uncleanness, lasciviousness,*
Galatians 5:20 Idolatry, witchcraft, hatred, variance, emulations, wrath, strife, seditions, heresies,
Galatians 5:21 Envyings, murders, drunkenness, revellings, and such like: of the which I tell you before, as I have also told [you] in time past, that **they which do such things shall not inherit the kingdom of God.**

Adultery	Hatred	Heresies
Fornication	Variance	Envying
Uncleanness	Emulation's	Murders
Lasciviousness	Wrath	Drunkenness
Idolatry	Strife	Reveling
Witchcraft	Sedition's	and the Like
6	6	6

Just in case you didn't think the list of traits in Galatians depicted you, God has in His infinite wisdom given us two separate descriptions of those that bear the mark. Keep in mind that most people will not display all of the characteristics listed. These are only the outward signs or manifestations of what's happening internally within the individual. The list is not intended to identify others but it should be used as a personal gauge to determine what type of witness is being given by our own life. Remember actions speak louder than words.

*2 Timothy 3:1 ¶ **This know also, that in the last days perilous times shall come.***

2 Timothy 3:2 For men shall be lovers of their own selves, covetous, boasters, proud, blasphemers, disobedient to parents, unthankful, unholy,

2 Timothy 3:3 Without natural affection, trucebreakers, false accusers, incontinent, fierce, despisers of those that are good,

2 Timothy 3:4 Traitors, heady, highminded, lovers of pleasures more than lovers of God;

lovers of themselves	unthankful	fierce
covetous	unholy	despisers of good
boasters	without love	Traitors
proud	trucebreakers	heady
blasphemers	false accusers	highminded
disobedient to parents	incontinent	lovers of pleasures - more than of God

6	**6**	**6**

God has not left us ignorant, wondering what is this mark of the beast? There is no reason to run around desperately hoping to identify it, so that we won't inadvertently receive it. Governments are not going to start branding us with some sort of identification for the antichrist. God has declared, that the works of the flesh (666) are evident (through examination), likewise so is the fruit of the Spirit (333). By using the descriptions above take some time to do an honest self-review, for you know in your heart whose mark you bear.

> **Note: The true meaning of the beast is man without God, so the mark of the beast is only a reflection of that fact.**

The good news is that the mark is not permanent. If you turn and give your heart to God (repentance), He will erase the mark and place His seal (salvation) upon you.

Chapter 16

The Announcements of the 3 Angels (Revelation 14:6-13)

And I saw another angel fly in the midst of heaven, having the everlasting gospel to preach unto them that dwell on the earth, and to every nation, and kindred, and tongue, and people.

Revelation 14:6

W hat we have here is a recapitulation of the main points of the tribulation period. God wants to impress upon us these 3 messages given by His angels; they have been echoed throughout Revelation. We need to hear what the Lord is saying here because this is the heart of the John's message and of the gospel itself. The first angel has the everlasting gospel of Jesus to deliver to the world. The second angel predicts the fall of Babylon. This statement is made in the past tense but it has not happened yet (prophesy). The third angel declares the punishment of all that receive the mark and worship the beast.

The first angel delivers the gospel (good news) to mankind, to be preached (proclaimed) to every nation, tribe, tongue and people. Here again God is using words and numbers to convey His point, the world is broken down into four different groups. The number 4 stands for all of creation or the world, the Word is to be published to every living person. Why, because the soul that sins will die, and we know that all have sinned and come short of the glory of God.

Therefore since man is a sinner by his very nature, we needed a remedy for sin. Jesus is God's solution to our problem; He has done what we are unable to do. Our sins have been laid upon Jesus and He has taken our place on Calvary's cross. We are now free from the debt of sin (death) and have life eternal through Christ. What do we pay for such a selfless act of love? God requires nothing of us; salvation is a free gift from God. He only asks that we acknowledge the work of His son in our lives.

No where else in history or religion do we see that a god has been willing to give up everything, in order to be a personal example of humility, love and sacrifice to His creation. When Jesus came to earth He suffered humiliation, rejection and death at the hands of mankind. Even today the Lord is willing to suffer rejection in order that some may be saved. Because of our (mankind's) sins we are predestined to death but God in His great mercy has offered us life. Don't delay any longer make your decision now.

The second angel announces the fall of Babylon, the great city. Babylon represents all that is worldly, carnal and sinful. It is in direct opposition to God's kingdom. Salvation means following God's way, Babylon means going the world's way. This prophecy is an indictment against the way of the world; God states that it will come to an end (fall). The Bible tells us that every knee shall bow and every tongue will confess that Jesus is Lord. That will be a time of great sadness for many, because that confession will be made too late. All that choose to live in Babylon (sin) will suffer eternal damnation.

Not only will those who choose to dwell in Babylon suffer separation (damnation) from God but they will also receive judgment for their actions. There will be different degrees of penalty's based on your sins, it will be a time of great sorrow and remorse. The first angel presented the eternal gospel; this angel shows us the final outcome of the world's system.

The last angel shows us the end results of rejecting the gospel and going the way of the world (Babylon). We have already established the mark of the beast is not literal but symbolic, just like the seal of God. The mark and the seal show ownership or affiliation. Anyone who has the seal of the Spirit does not have the mark of the beast and vice versa. There are only two sides to the coin; there are only two forces present in the world good and evil. If we are not of God, then we are of the devil. Either we serve the Lord or we serve Satan. Am I being too severe, is it really that black and white?

> *Romans 6:16* ***Know ye not, that to whom ye yield yourselves*** *servants to obey, his servants ye are to whom ye obey;* ***whether of sin unto death, or of obedience unto righteousness?***

> *Matthew6:24* ***No man can serve two masters:*** *for either* ***he will hate the one, and love the other;*** *or else* ***he will hold to the one, and despise the other.*** *Ye cannot serve God and mammon.*

Robert R. Davis

Clearly the bible teaches that there are only two sides and we must choose either one or the other. Whenever you are presented with the gospel you are making a choice, either consciously or unconsciously. All who reject God will suffer the consequences of their actions; they will experience the fullness of His wrath.

The last two verses in the chapter advises the saints to have patience and this has been echoed throughout Revelation. Why, because sin, wickedness and tribulation will increase and chaos will start to reign. It will seem like the wicked will never be punished. The natural inclination is to give up and say what's the use. Especially when you see those without God prospering but you are serving Him and struggling, it's very easy to feel discouraged. But the Lord is saying to His people, hold on because what you see is not the end of things.

> *Psalms 37:7 ¶ Rest in the LORD, and wait patiently for him: **fret not thyself because of him who prospereth in his way**, because of the man who bringeth wicked devices to pass.*
>
> *Psalms 37:8 Cease from anger, and forsake wrath: fret not thyself in any wise to do evil.*
>
> *Psalms 37:9 **For evildoers shall be cut off: but those that wait upon the LORD, they shall inherit the earth.***

God will judge and pay everyone for his or her actions (works) whether they are good or bad. Let me emphasize that being a good person is not enough because good works cannot save us. Salvation is through accepting (faith in) Jesus; our good works attract others to God and are used to determine our rewards after redemption.

To summarize, we must first make a choice of whom we will serve because our choice determines our eternal destination. Then after that our works will dictate what our rewards or punishments will be.

Chapter 17

The Little Book
(Revelation 10)

And I took the little book out of the angel's hand, and ate it up; and it was in my mouth sweet as honey: and as soon as I had eaten it, my belly was bitter.

And he said unto me, Thou must prophesy again before many peoples, and nations, and tongues, and kings.

Revelation 10:10,11

Here we see a mighty angel that represents Christ; note the things that pertained to Christ. A face like the sun, the cloud, feet like a pillar of fire. The little book is the prophecy (the book of Revelation) that John must proclaim to us. This vision contrasts the ministry of Ezekiel to John's prophetic office. Judgment and restoration are the main focus of both ministries. Even the purpose is the same, the Lord's objective in judging the world is not simply punishing the wicked but to bring mankind to repentance.

A strange event occurs during this vision, when Christ (the mighty angel) speaks 7 thunders utter their voices. John was about to write what was said but he is told to seal up what was uttered and not to write it. Everything in the book of Revelation is supposed to be open, which is the very implication of the title itself. Why are the messages from the 7 thunders hidden and their judgments sealed?

The seven thunders would have prolonged the tribulation period, perhaps to the point where the faithful Christians would have given up. The 7 thunders would have followed the 7 trumpets in sequence but now all delay has been removed and the 7th trumpet will be the final step in the great tribulation. What the seven thunders uttered may forever remain a mystery but the Lord in His infinite wisdom has chosen not to postpone His coming any longer.

Remember the 5th seal and souls under the altar, crying out to God. *"How long O Lord, holy and true, dost thou not judge and avenge our blood on them that dwell on the earth?"* We are quickly climaxing to that point, the 7th trumpet will usher in the wrath of God. Not only that but we are told that the mystery of God will be finished, when the last trumpet sounds. What exactly is the mystery of God?

The mystery of God is His plan of salvation through Jesus Christ, it is literally the kingdom of God. The essence of the mystery is this "That the Gentiles should be fellow heirs, and of the same body, and partakers of his promise through Christ by the gospel" This is common knowledge to us now but to the Jews this is still not accepted as truth. Still the question remains how will the 7th trumpet finish the mystery of God?

> *1 Corinthians 15:51 ¶* ***Behold, I shew you a mystery;*** *We shall not all sleep, but we shall all be changed,*
> *1 Corinthians 15:52 In a moment, in the twinkling of an eye,* ***at the last trump: for the trumpet shall sound, and the dead shall be raised incorruptible, and we shall be changed.***

The rapture or resurrection of the church is the last step in the mystery of God. Fantastic as that may sound, this is central to the hope of the gospel of Christ. The apostle Paul put it this way in Corinthians

> *1 Corinthians 15:16 For if the dead rise not, then is not Christ raised:*
> *1 Corinthians 15:17 And if Christ be not raised, your faith is vain; ye are yet in your sins.*
> *1 Corinthians 15:18 Then they also which are fallen asleep in Christ are perished.*
> *1 Corinthians 15:19* ***If in this life only we have hope in Christ, we are of all men most miserable.***

Still the question remains why is this vision here, if this vision only speaks of John's having to give this prophecy (the book of Revelation), I would say that it doesn't belong here. For we already hold John as a prophet and we realize that this book is a prophecy from God. So why put the vision in between the 6th and 7th trumpets?

What John has told us to this point is basically historical fact; although we gain great spiritual insights from these visions so far they deal with only the past and present. The visions to this point come under the category of the "spirit of revelation" or "word of knowledge". From the 7th trumpet on we move into the realm of prophecy or foretelling the future. This vision not only breaks up the 6th and 7th trumpets but it shows us a shift in emphasis from historical facts to future events. We can clearly pinpoint where we stand today in relation to the timeline of Revelation.

There is only one more mystery that we still need to solve. When the final trumpet is sounded, will you be ready?

Robert R. Davis

The Future

- The 7th Trumpet
- The Lamb and the 144,000
- The Harvest Judgment
- The Great Multitude
- Satan Released
- The 7 Bowls
- The Great Harlot
- Babylon the Great
- The Battle of Armageddon
- The Marriage Supper of the Lamb
- The Great White Throne Judgment
- The New Heaven and Earth

Robert R. Davis

Chapter 18

The 7ᵗʰ Trumpet
(Revelation 11:15-19)

And the seventh angel sounded; and there were great voices in heaven, saying, The kingdoms of this world are become *the kingdoms* of our Lord, and of his Christ; and he shall reign for ever and ever.

Revelation 11:15

When the seventh trumpet is sounded, heaven will proclaim that the kingdoms of the world have become God's and Christ's. The mystery of God will be finished, the rapture has taken place and the wrath of God (3ʳᵈ Woe) will now begin. This is the third and final woe; it will start a time of suffering that has been predicted from antiquity, the great and terrible day of the Lord.

1ˢᵗ Woe - Satan being cast down to the earth
2ⁿᵈ Woe - The Great Tribulation
3ʳᵈ Woe - Wrath of God

How will Christ gain control over the kingdoms of the world through the 7ᵗʰ trumpet? When the trumpet is sounded the church (true believers) will be gathered together to the Lord. The church consists of people from every nation on the earth, so through the church the kingdoms of this world will become Christ's. Satan will still be ruling in the earthly realm temporarily.

There are grave implications associated to the last trumpet, which lead ultimately to judgment. For example the church represents the living embodiment of the truth (Word of God). The world without this voice proclaiming the truth will be subject to mass deception. Chaos and anarchy will reign; a dark New World will emerge. The stage is now being set for this to happen, so when it does it won't be a major shock. We have already seen that the moral restraint of the church has been removed (killed).

With the church out of the way Satan will have free reign to control the earth unhampered. Governments will be mere puppets for the adversary without the restraining influence of the church praying for God's intervention. Man will become an even greater enemy to himself, causing more self-induced suffering than ever before.

One would think that an event as great as the 7th trumpet would cause everyone to immediately turn to God. Sadly most still will not repent or even see what happens as an act of God. Some catastrophic event must occur during that time, to cause people to doubt the validity of the rapture. A great earthquake is prophesied, perhaps in more than one region. The fact that many who are believed to be Christians will still be here, may lead others to disallow the resurrection of the church.

After the 7th trumpet is sounded God's temple is opened and the Ark of the Covenant is seen, what is the significance of this symbol? By allowing us to see the Ark of the Covenant, God is illustrating that Christ our high priest has completed His ministry of atonement for our sins and the temple (our bodies) has been cleansed. Now that the saints have received their final atonement the wrath of God will commence judgment upon those left on the earth. The day of the Lord or the wrath of God has been predicted since the time of prophets. In the 5th seal we saw the Old Testament saints pleading with God to avenge them. Israel thought the Messiah would fulfill this role in his 1st advent but they did not understand God's full plan of salvation. When Christ comes for His church during the rapture (2nd Advent), then He will destroy His enemies and exact vengeance upon the earth.

Even in the day of God's wrath, the Lord is calling mankind to repentance. Undoubtedly people will give their hearts to the Lord during this time but they will have to endure the time of God's wrath. That will be a grievous hardship because the day of wrath is not intended for the believer. If Christians barely make it in this dispensation (grace), how will they endure during His wrath? This brings to light the true meaning of Jesus words; "Blessed and holy is he who has part in the first resurrection (rapture)"[39]. May all that read this book be part of the 1st resurrection, which the second death has no power.

Chapter 19

The Lamb and the 144,000
(Revelation 14:1-5)

**And I looked, and, lo, a Lamb stood on the mount
Sion, and with him an hundred forty *and* four thousand,
having his Father's name written in their foreheads.**

Revelation 14:1

The 144,000 pictured here are the same that was sealed back in
Revelation chapter 7; they are the firstfruits of God and the
Lamb. The firstfruits of your labor (produce or crop) were
given to the Lord before the full harvest was gathered. Firstfruits were
presents made to God to express submission, dependence and thankfulness.
They were offered in the temple before the crop (full harvest) was gathered.
Salvation was initially promised to Israel (Jews) here we see the Old
Testament saints being offered to God as a token of submission by Christ
Jesus. God made a provision for His priest to receive the firstfruits as an
inheritance.

> *Hebrews 4:14 Seeing then that we have a **great high
> priest**, that is passed into the heavens, **Jesus the Son of God**,
> let us hold fast our profession.*

Jesus is our high priest therefore the firstfruits are also given to Him for
an inheritance, this is how the 144,000 become the firstfruits of God and the
Lamb. That's why they follow the Lamb wherever He goes and the rest of
the church is not mentioned. This is also the reason the sealing of the
144,000 was mentioned and not the sealing of all of the saints of God. It's
not that all of God's people aren't sealed because they are; this was done to
emphasize the special place of the 144,000 as the firstfruits to the Lord.

The 144,000 (firstfruits) are naturally reaped before the harvest
judgment and that is why they are placed here. By showing us the hundred
and forty four thousand of Israel again we are being given clues to help us

91

identify the 144,000 as the firstfruits. Remember that the firstfruits were actually gathered when Jesus was resurrected; by placing them here we can draw a clear connection between the 144,000 and the great multitude of Gentiles. Now we are ready for the full harvest to be gathered together.

Chapter 20

The Harvest Judgment
(Revelation 14:14-20)

And I looked, and behold a white cloud, and upon the cloud *one* sat like unto the Son of man, having on his head a golden crown, and in his hand a sharp sickle.

And another angel came out of the temple, crying with a loud voice to him that sat on the cloud, Thrust in thy sickle, and reap: for the time is come for thee to reap; for the harvest of the earth is ripe.

Revelation 14:14,15

The Son of man (Jesus) is pictured on a cloud ready to gather the harvest of the earth. Here we see symbolic language used to describe what we refer to, in the church, as the rapture. The rapture is a gathering together of the Lord's people both dead and alive to Himself. It is the last step in the mystery of the kingdom of God. The harvest judgment is the same event as the 7th trumpet and the 2nd Advent of the Messiah.

As we stated before the rapture of the church is central to the hope of the gospel. Also we found that the church (2 witnesses) is actually fulfilling the ministry of Christ, having 3 ½ years to proclaim God's word. After that the church will be killed and remain dead for 3 ½ days, then they will be resurrected and ascended into heaven. So Jesus is our example and pattern not only in living this life but also in our resurrection.

It seems plausible to us that Jesus could ascend into heaven, after all He is the Son of God but the entire church disappearing at one time stretches our imagination. Thankfully, God has given us other examples of the rapture experience. Enoch who was the seventh (symbolic of all) man was translated (raptured) into heaven. Also Elijah was carried into heaven by a whirlwind and a chariot of fire (Holy Spirit).

> *Hebrews 11:5 By faith Enoch was translated that he should not see death; and was not found, because God had translated him: for before his translation he had this testimony, that he pleased God.*
>
> *2 Kings 2:11 And it came to pass, as they still went on, and talked, that, behold, there appeared a chariot of fire, and horses of fire, and parted them both asunder; and Elijah went up by a whirlwind into heaven.*

Enoch, Elijah and Jesus here we have three that bear witness to us that the rapture is indeed a credible doctrine. Let's take a look at the scriptures and see if it also bears witness to the rapture theory.

> *1 Corinthians 15:51 ¶ Behold, I shew you a mystery; We shall not all sleep, but we shall all be changed,*
> *1 Corinthians 15:52 In a moment, in the twinkling of an eye, at the last trump: for the trumpet shall sound, and the dead shall be raised incorruptible, and we shall be changed.*

All Christians that are familiar with the rapture know this passage. Paul mentions a trumpet, not only that but the sounding of the last trumpet, then the rapture will occur. In Revelation after the seventh and last trumpet is sounded, the rapture of the church occurs. Is this a coincidence, Corinthians was written approx. 40 years prior to the book of Revelation? The linkage here and other places points to the authorship and inspiration of the Holy Spirit in writing the Bible. That's just my opinion you certainly don't have to agree with that. Let's look at another scripture because we need another witness to establish this as a fact.

> *Matthew 24:29 Immediately after the tribulation of those days shall the sun be darkened, and the moon shall not give her light, and the stars shall fall from heaven, and the powers of the heavens shall be shaken:*
> *Matthew 24:30 And then shall appear the sign of the Son of man in heaven: and then shall all the tribes of the earth mourn, and they shall see the Son of man coming in the clouds of heaven with power and great glory.*

*Matthew 24:31 And he shall send his angels with a **great
sound of a trumpet**, and they shall **gather together his elect**
from the four winds, from one end of heaven to the other.*

Here we have Jesus Himself speaking this time, He says that after the
tribulation (the Great Tribulation) He will come on the clouds with power
and glory. His angels will gather together His elect at the sound of the
trumpet. There's that trumpet again another coincidence? Also note that
Jesus (the Son of Man) is on the clouds, just like in Revelation. The rapture
of the church is the Second Coming of Christ. The first advent was
physical; the second is spiritual. The Lord's first coming was to administer
salvation to mankind, when He comes again it will be to execute judgment
in the earth.

Let's look at two examples so that we might understand the need for the
rapture before God's judgment. The first is Noah and the second is Lot
(Sodom and Gomorrah). Why these two, because in both cases man was
destroyed by the wrath of God. The story of Noah is familiar to most; God
destroyed the world because of the wickedness of mankind (this was a
prelude to the end time). Only eight people were saved from destruction via
the ark. These eight did not experience God's wrath, incidentally eight is
the number for resurrection[40].

Noah was counted righteous according to God and was spared from the
destruction of the flood. The Lord could have, very well started from
scratch and remade mankind but Noah was found righteous and did not
deserve God's wrath.

Now let's look at Lot, God spoke to Abraham and divulged His plan to
destroy the city. Abraham pleaded with God on the city's behalf; notice
what he said about the Lord.

*Genesis 18:23 And Abraham drew near, and said, **Wilt
thou also destroy the righteous with the wicked?***
*Genesis 18:24 Peradventure there be fifty righteous
within the city: wilt thou also destroy and not spare the place
for the fifty righteous that [are] therein?*
*Genesis 18:25 That be far from thee to do after this
manner, to slay the righteous with the wicked: and that the
righteous should be as the wicked, that be far from thee:
Shall not the Judge of all the earth do right?*

Did you grasp the significance of what Abraham said to God? The
righteous would be counted as the wicked if God were to destroy them.

95

Abraham declares that God would not be doing right, if He destroyed the righteous along with the wicked. To that we would have to echo Abraham's words, far be it from you, Lord. We know that God could have easily destroyed Sodom and Gomorrah without recreating man but He will not punish the righteous along with the wicked. Therefore it is absolutely critical that the rapture occur before the wrath of God can be administered.

It is astonishing to think that an event the size of the rapture will not cause every living soul to repent. But as I said before there has to be some major catastrophe that will cause people to miss this remarkable sign. A great earthquake is prophesied in some texts and in this vision blood comes up to the height of the horses' bridles and covers approximately 184 miles. When the harvest is reaped there will be an incident that causes major carnage. Most likely people will associate the disappearances of the saints on whatever this calamity happens to be.

I believe we have clearly seen that God will not allow His saints to endure His wrath, which is reserved for the wicked. Then this milestone, which is the final mystery of God (the rapture), must be a literal event and afterwards the wrath of God will be poured out upon the earth.

Concerning the resurrection of the church Jesus Himself admonishes us, "Watch therefore, for ye know neither the day nor the hour wherein the Son of man cometh[41]".

Chapter 21

The Great Multitude
(Revelation 7:9-17)

After this I beheld, and, lo, a great multitude, which no man could number, of all nations, and kindreds, and people, and tongues, stood before the throne, and before the Lamb, clothed with white robes, and palms in their hands;

Revelation 7:9

Here we see the great multitude from every nation, this is the full harvest of the church. It was confusing to have this vision placed between the 6th and 7th seals, because this event doesn't actually occur until after the 7th trumpet. But the firstfruits and the great multitude naturally belong together, in order to see that they are from the same harvest. This multitude consists of the New Testament saints that have died and those that were translated (raptured) during the great tribulation. They have washed their robes and made them white through the blood of the Lamb (salvation through faith).

The multitude are holding palm branches in their hands, this is symbolic of Christ coming into His kingdom. In the gospel of St. John we have a physical prelude to this spiritual event. It is significant enough for all four gospel writers to record this blessed event.

*St. John 12:13 Took **branches of palm trees**, and went forth to meet him, and **cried, Hosanna**: Blessed is the King of Israel that cometh in the name of the Lord.*

This time Christ is truly coming into His kingdom and all of heaven will cry out Hosanna, blessed is He that comes in the name of the Lord. Hosanna literally means save now, Christ has come and resurrected His people as their deliverer. This will be an unparalleled time of celebration and rejoicing in heaven, because through Christ we have received the victory. There will be no more sorrow, sickness, hunger or thirst, for God will cloth us in our new resurrected bodies. We will finally see God face to face and we will know Him as He know us. I don't think anyone can fully comprehend the beauty, riches and the glory that the Lord has prepared for those that overcome.

Let me be clear here, there are only two resurrections. The first resurrection consists of Israel and the church and the second gathers all the remaining people both living and dead. The 144,000 (Israel) are included in the first resurrection. The firstfruits are gathered and offered to the Lord, then the rest of the crop is gathered but they are both taken from the same harvest. All of the fruit from the first harvest is good but the second harvest must be separated. This is why it says, "Blessed and holy is he who has part in the first resurrection". Everyone included in the rapture will have his or her name written in the Book of Life but that's not the case with the second resurrection. All who are in the 2nd resurrection must appear before the judgment seat of God, to determine their final destination and rewards or punishments.

When we first started viewing the rapture or resurrection it seemed to be a rather fantastic theory but as we can see everyone will experience a resurrection. **The question is not will you be resurrected but rather which one will you take part in?**

Chapter 22

Satan Released
(Revelation 20:7-10)

And when the thousand years are expired, Satan shall be loosed out of his prison.

And shall go out to deceive the nations which are in the four quarters of the earth, Gog and Magog, to gather them together to battle: the number of whom *is* as the sand of the sea.

Revelation 20:7,8

After Satan is loosed he will also deceive the nations of the world into gathering for war against the beloved city Jerusalem. This is another description of the sixth bowl or the battle of Armageddon. The camp of the saints mentioned is a reference to the restored state of Israel. As I stated previously it is probable that the rapture will lead the Jews to believe that Jesus is the Messiah. The rapture of the church will loose Satan, since the church is the embodiment of Christ (the truth).

After Satan is released then the world will experience untold suffering, because he realizes that God's physical kingdom is imminent and he will do anything he can to stop it. This will be the final round for the adversary and he knows it, he will unleash a fury of demonic attacks upon mankind like never before. He will cause man to sink to his most base level; humanity will be deceived, seduced and harassed to commit every sin imaginable. Consequently this will have a reciprocal effect, the increase in sin will help fuel the wrath of God.

The battle of Armageddon (Gog and Magog) will be the last and final battle of mankind. This is the historic site of many battles and it is the setting for the final Great War. The battle of Armageddon is really about the spiritual warfare between our Lord and Satan for the soul of man. This is Satan's last stand before his ultimate defeat. Since the church has been raptured and won the victory, he has focused his anger on Israel (The

99

Woman). But God will also give Israel the victory, bringing this age to an end. Then everyone both dead and alive will be resurrected (2nd and final), to appear before God's throne for judgment.

In this vision we also see Satan's final fate, it is with the beast and the false prophet in the lake of fire. There they will be tormented perpetually both night and day. But this shouldn't be the fate of mankind, because hell wasn't created for us. That's the reason that God has gone through such great lengths to redeem man back unto Himself. It's not God who puts us in hell, where we spend eternity is of our own volition.

Chapter 23

The 7 Bowls
(Revelations 15 & 16)

Preparation for the bowls

> **And I saw another sign in heaven, great and marvellous, seven angels having the seven last plagues; for in them is filled up the wrath of God.**
> **And I saw as it were a sea of glass mingled with fire: and them that had gotten the victory over the beast, and over his image, and over his mark, *and* over the number of his name, stand on the sea of glass, having the harps of God.**

> ***Revelation 15:1,2***

Here we have yet another sign in heaven, this is the 3rd and last great sign in the book of Revelation. The first was the woman about to give birth; this represented Israel bringing forth the Messiah. The second was the great red dragon being cast out of heaven; the power and authority given to the church was emblematic of this. This last sign shows seven angels with the last 7 plagues. The only visible sign of that on earth will be the rapture itself, when the remaining people see this event it should be a clear signal that the wrath of God is ready to begin.

*St. Matthew 24:30 And then **shall appear the sign of the Son of man in heaven**: and then shall all the tribes of the earth mourn, and they shall see the Son of man **coming in the clouds of heaven** with power and great glory.*

1st Sign - The Virgin Mary giving birth to the Messiah
2nd Sign - The authority given to the Church through Christ
3rd Sign - The rapture or 2nd Advent of Christ

It is interesting to note, that Satan and the effects of sin have caused the 3 woes to occur. But in contrast Jesus and the results of righteousness are the source the 3 great signs in the earth. Every sign has a two-pronged effect bringing with it both blessing and curses (woes). The first sign, the coming of the Messiah caused the devil to be cast out of heaven (1st woe). The second sign, the authority given to the church has started an all out war in the earth specifically the Great Tribulation (2nd woe). The third and last sign, the rapture or resurrection of the church ushers in the dreaded wrath of God (3rd woe).

Next notice those who overcome (the saints) are standing by the sea of glass, the sea represents multitudes of peoples from all nations and the fire depicts the judgment of the world. The fact that the saints or those who were victorious over the beast are standing at the sea of glass points to them ruling over the nations and standing in judgment with Christ.

1 Corinthians 6:2 ***Do ye not know that the saints shall
judge the world?*** *and if the world shall be judged by you,
are ye unworthy to judge the smallest matters?*

Both Israel (Old Testament saints) and the Church will judge the nations with the Lord; the songs indicate this, they sing one of Moses and one of the Lamb. Please, note if any Israelite (Jew) receives the seal of God after the resurrection of Christ, then they would be included in the great multitude (church) not Israel. Israel's number the 144,000, although it's not a literal number, is final (closed); anyone else that is added to the kingdom will be appended to the great multitude (the church) regardless of his or her heritage.

We see the tabernacle of testimony (the temple) is opened in heaven, which symbolizes that atonement has been made for God's people by the high priest (Jesus Christ). The work of Christ covers every believer in the body (the Church) just like the high priest did for the whole congregation of Israel. At this point the true church has received atonement and been raptured, everyone else will experience the wrath of God. God's glory (smoke) fills the temple and no one can enter until the 7 plagues are completed. This is reminiscent of His Old Testament dealings with Israel, while God's glory fills the temple all of heaven waits till this work is completed. We can see the seriousness of these last plagues, for the Lord has entered His temple and will not be appeased until His wrath has been fully poured out.

1ˢᵗ Bowl

And the first went, and poured out his vial upon the earth; and there fell a noisome and grievous sore upon the men which had the mark of the beast, and *upon* them which worshipped his image.

Revelation 16:2

As we already know at this point the church has been raptured. We see that God is ready to pour out His judgment upon the earth. When the first bowl or vial is poured out, foul and loathsome sores appear on mankind. What are these sores exactly and what are their causes we are not told, they are reminiscent of the plagues God placed upon Pharaoh and Egypt.

> *Exodus 9:8 And the LORD said unto Moses and unto Aaron, Take to you handfuls of ashes of the furnace, and let Moses sprinkle it toward the heaven in the sight of Pharaoh.*
> *Exodus 9:9 And it shall become small dust in all the land of Egypt, and shall be **a boil breaking forth [with] blains upon man**, and upon beast, throughout all the land of Egypt.*
> *Exodus 9:10 And they took ashes of the furnace, and stood before Pharaoh; and Moses sprinkled it up toward heaven; and it became a boil breaking forth [with] blains upon man, and upon beast.*
> *Exodus 9:11 And the magicians could not stand before Moses because of the boils; for the boil was upon the magicians, and upon all the Egyptians.*

In the book of Exodus only the Egyptian's were affected by this plague in the same way those who have the mark of the beast will receive these boils. Egypt symbolizes the world without God or worldliness, just like the beast of the sea. One difference to note about this plague is the saints have already been taken from the earth. So there will not be a distinction made between believer and a non-believer, due to the rapture of the church.

There is no need to speculate on exactly what this boil represents, it could be anything from an airborne virus to a chemical reaction. We do know that it will be a grievous sore to the people that acquire it and that could be all of mankind.

2ⁿᵈ Bowl

And the second angel poured out his vial upon the sea; and it became as the blood of a dead *man*: and every living soul died in the sea.

Revelation 16:3

This bowl appears to be a continuation and culmination of the 2nd Trumpet. In the second trumpet 1/3 of all of the sea life was destroyed, this was physically carried out by the hand of man. Obviously man will continue to pollute the waters with toxins, oil and other contaminates. Having no life in the sea is almost unimaginable. This plague will wreck havoc with the earth's ecology system and the whole balance of nature.

Since this bowl or plague is actually a gradual succession of the 2nd trumpet, most will not recognize its spiritual origins. It will be a natural progression of what has already been started today. Remember Satan will be free to deceive all on the earth at this time, so most people will probably look at the scientific or environmental factors that contribute to this dilemma.

One of the main problems man has today, in recognizing the signs of God is that we usually want some dramatic event to occur. Unfortunately the Lord doesn't split the seas every time He wants our attention, most of the time He uses everyday occurrences to accomplish His will and Word. So it's very important to know God's Word, in order to recognize the various ways it is fulfilled.

3ʳᵈ Bowl

And the third angel poured out his vial upon the rivers and fountains of waters; and they became blood.

Revelation 16:4

Like the previous vision this bowl is also a continuation and culmination of its counterpart the 3rd Trumpet. All drinking water has become unusable and contaminated, water is absolutely vital to not only man's existence but to all life. Already there are countries where the water must be purified before you can drink it, this evidently will become a worldwide situation. The world will soon be in a very critical situation, it will not sit still at 1/3 of the drinking water being contaminated. Once the 3rd trumpet is fulfilled the process just continues until we reach a 100% (3rd bowl).

This plague is so severe that an angel speaks out saying, "the Lord is righteous, for you have given them blood to drink and this is their just do"[42]. Yet another angel proclaims the righteousness of God in executing His judgments in the earth. Based on the reaction in heaven, many will suffer and die from this plague.

Again, we must remember the point of all of this is not just retribution but more importantly it is designed to be one last chance for man to repent (turn to God). Unfortunately the reaction of most will be the same as Pharaoh of Egypt; they will harden their hearts (remain unrepentant). Even so, God still gives man the opportunity to escape the reality of experiencing the second death or eternal separation.

4th Bowl

And the fourth angel poured out his vial upon the sun; and power was given unto him to scorch men with fire.

And men were scorched with great heat, and blasphemed the name of God, which hath power over these plagues: and they repented not to give him glory.

Revelation 16:8,9

This bowl seems to differ from the pattern of the first three trumpets in that instead of a continuing and total darkening of the sun, the sun's rays begins to scorch men. The 4th trumpet depicted a darkening of the sun, probably through regional haze. In reality this is a continuation of the 4th trumpet; although the symptoms are different, the causes are the same. It appears that the factors that contributed to the hazing effect (dimming of natural light) will eventually cause the sun to sear mankind. Here we see the possibility of a total erosion of the earth's ozone layer. Although it's not mentioned directly the combination of no viable drinking water and the burning heat (global warming) probably wipes out scores of people and animals.

The ozone layer is critically important to man because it protects life on earth from the full force of the sun's cancer-causing ultraviolet radiation. Destruction of the ozone layer will cause a myriad of problems such as:

- Skin cancer
- Cataracts
- Damage to crops
- Increased carbon dioxide (global warming)

Some common culprits of the ozone's depletion are aerosol dispensers, air pollution, fluorine, nuclear weapons and refrigeration. Just because science can tell us the factors that cause the ozone predicament, tracing the origins of these problems back to man. The fact still remains that the Bible predicted these occurrences long before we even knew there was an ozone.

As I said before these events will not happen suddenly but they are slowly developing, the world is becoming warmer and wetter (humidity). That may relate to changes in ENSO (El Nino Southern Oscillation). Burning of coal, wood, oil, gasoline and other fossil fuels has increased the level of carbon dioxide in the atmosphere. Many scientists believe that carbon dioxide and other human produced 'greenhouse' gases have adversely affected the world's climate."[43] The Bible states that in spite of all of the misery and suffering being experienced, people will still not repent.

Note: If you do repent during this time period you will still have to endure the plagues of this dispensation, since the church has already been raptured.

What about those who are born after the rapture? It would probably be prudent during this time period not to have children, due to the suffering that will be experienced but naturally people will continue to reproduce.

> *Matthew 24:33 So likewise ye, when ye shall see all these things, know that it is near, even at the doors.*
> *Matthew 24:34 Verily I say unto you, **This generation shall not pass, till all these things be fulfilled.***

Luckily this will be the last generation to experience such misery. Jesus said that when you see these things (the rapture) know that the end is near. For the current generation will not pass away before God's wrath is completed. A generation is the average span of time between the birth of parents and that of their offspring[44].

5ᵗʰ Bowl

And the fifth angel poured out his vial upon the seat of the beast; and his kingdom was full of darkness; and they gnawed their tongues for pain, And blasphemed the God of heaven because of their pains and their sores, and repented not of their deeds.

Revelation 16:10,11

Here we see that the seat or throne of the beast is covered in darkness, darkness is symbolic of misery and adversity. What kingdom or country symbolizes the beast during this particular time is unknown, but we do know that Satan is the influencing power behind it. The enemy's headquarters is shown to be greatly suffering from the effects of these plagues.

The people blaspheme God because of their miseries, how ironic since their sins are the real causes of their pain and not God. The Lord desires that these plagues turn men back to Him; instead they curse their only source of help. Look how greatly the enemy has deceived these people!

Even today we have that same mindset, hurricanes, floods and tornadoes are called acts of God. Satan is the ruler of this present world and the author of most of its misery but who gets blamed for all the wrong? If lighting strikes your house and it burns to the ground, the insurance company will classify it as an act of God. Now why would God want to burn down your house and leave you empty? That's an act of the Devil, not God. The birth of your children is truly an act of God.

The problem we have here is the same one we have had throughout the ages, "the god of this world hath blinded the minds of them, which believe not, lest the light of the glorious gospel of Christ, who is the image of God, should shine unto them"[45]. The situation will be much worse after the rapture since the adversary will be virtually unrestrained.

6ᵗʰ Bowl

And the sixth angel poured out his vial upon the great river Euphrates; and the water thereof was dried up, that the way of the kings of the east might be prepared.

Revelation 16:12

In this bowl the spirit of deception is loosed upon the earth to deceive the nations and to gather them for war. Next to the number 666, the battle of Armageddon is one of the most widely known events in Revelation. The number six we know stands for man but it also seems to indicate aggression or attacks. In the 6th seal we saw the physical and spiritual aggression towards our Lord (Jesus), resulting in His crucifixion. The 6th trumpet gave us insight into the spiritual warfare that had been initiated upon man. This 6th bowl is foretelling the commencement of the final battle (Armageddon) in the Holy Land.

The Euphrates River will dry up; this will allow the kings of the east to cross over into the Holy Land. This may or may not be a physical occurrence but it signifies that these kings or kingdoms (countries) will now have free access to cross over into Israel. At the present time the countries east of the Euphrates River are Arab or Muslim, the Israeli's and the Arabs have been rivals for years. We can discern from the spirits of deception that are loosed, that Satan has always been at the root of the problems in the Middle East.

This will literally be a war to end all wars, at its end the earth will be destroyed. All of this destruction over one parcel of land, Israel has been one of the most fought over pieces of real estate in the history of mankind. The Muslims claim it as their Holy Land and of course the Jews voice the same claim. When looking at things from the human perspective, it just doesn't make sense but we must remember that there are spiritual implications to this constant fighting.

It is prophesied that the Messiah will come again to restore the kingdom to Israel. He will bring a time of peace and prosperity never before enjoyed by the land. This same parcel of land (New Jerusalem) has been promised to believers as part of their inheritance with Christ. The true restoration of Israel will only occur in the kingdom of God, there will not be a time of peace in this age. This prophecy[46] will only be fulfilled in the new Heaven and earth, after our bodies have been regenerated. Satan cannot stop the restoration of Israel, so he works to prevent us from receiving the blessings of our inheritance.

> *Galatians 3:13* **Christ hath redeemed us** *from the curse of the law, being made a curse for us: for it is written, Cursed is every one that hangeth on a tree:*
> *Galatians 3:14* **That the blessing of Abraham might come on the Gentiles** *through Jesus Christ; that we might receive the promise of the Spirit through faith.*

Because God has promised this land in His Word, the adversary will do anything to stop us from receiving it. We have already seen through the work of Christ on Calvary that Satan is a defeated foe. He cannot stop the promises or work of God and his end has already been prophesied.

Our objective then is to overcome Satan so that he doesn't stop us from receiving the promises of God.

Before this vision closes the Lord interrupts with a message to mankind. This is the only plague where Christ interjects, there is enormous significance attached to this fact. Jesus Himself speaks a warning to be alert and watch. This is one last call to repentance and it is given directly from the Lord.

> *Revelation 16:15 Behold, I come as a thief. Blessed is he that watcheth, and keepeth his garments, lest he walk naked, and they see his shame.*

This is the final warning or sign, because after this bowl is poured out we have the culmination of God's wrath in the 7th and the last bowl. Armageddon is the final conflict and literally man's last opportunity to turn to God.

7th Bowl

> **And the seventh angel poured out his vial into the air; and there came a great voice out of the temple of heaven, from the throne, saying, It is done.**

> ***Revelation 16:17***

Notice that there is no gap between the 6th and the 7th bowls as there was with the seals and the trumpets. That's because God is in His temple and nothing will distract Him until His wrath is finished. We know that Armageddon has already begun; this is a war that will threaten to annihilate all of humanity. There will be earthquakes and great hailstones (up to 75 lbs.) it is possible that the hailstones are the cause of the earthquakes. One possible scenario could be that a meteor or meteors would hit the earth.

There was a movie depicting such a scenario in graphic detail and it was titled of all things "Armageddon".

Just as Jesus said on the cross "It is finished" speaking of His work of salvation, God states "It is done" concerning His act of judgment. This 7th bowl culminates with the end of the battle of Armageddon, resulting in the dissolution of the world, as we know it. An earthquake of greater magnitude than has ever been recorded, will rock the earth and whole cities will collapse due to its enormity. Here we see the fulfillment of the last part of the 6th seal.

> *Revelation 6:15 And the kings of the earth, and the great men, and the rich men, and the chief captains, and the mighty men, and every bondman, and every free man, hid themselves in the dens and in the rocks of the mountains;*
>
> *Revelation 6:16 And said to the mountains and rocks, Fall on us, and* **hide us from the face of him that sitteth on the throne***, and from the wrath of the Lamb:*
>
> *Revelation 6:17* **For the great day of his wrath is come; and who shall be able to stand?**

This will be an unprecedented time of calamity and misery; humanity will suffer globally because of their sins and mainly by their own hands. Man apart from God will self-destruct; because the absence of God is the absence of love. Without love man will turn savagely and mercilessly upon his fellow man, in a futile quest for domination and superiority.

The great city will be divided into 3 parts, her remembrance will go up before God and He will pour out the fierceness of His wrath. The city that John is referring to is Babylon the great. She is punished because the blood of the prophets and saints was found in her. So notable are her sins before God that the city is singled out to receive direct punishment from the Lord. We will go into more detail about Babylon later in the book; because of her long history of atrocious deeds the Lord dedicates almost 3 chapters of Revelation to her destruction.

This last bowl will cause the islands and the mountains to be obliterated, note that mountains represent kingdoms. So these events will cause kingdoms or counties to dissipate, remember the declaration of the 7th trumpet; "the kingdoms of this world have become the kingdoms of our Lord and His Christ..." Now we are preparing to see the physical manifestation of this heavenly pronouncement. God's great wrath is now completed and all of the remaining inhabitants of the earth both dead and alive will be resurrected (2nd resurrection), to await the final judgment of God.

Chapter 24

The Great Harlot
(Revelation 17)

The great harlot described

> **And there came one of the seven angels which had the seven vials, and talked with me, saying unto me, Come hither; I will shew unto thee the judgment of the great whore that sitteth upon many waters:**
> **With whom the kings of the earth have committed fornication, and the inhabitants of the earth have been made drunk with the wine of her fornication.**

Revelation 17:1,2

The seventh bowl has been poured out and God's wrath has been completed. But now we have the great harlot being described to us, where does this fit in? John is filling in some details about the 2 beasts we saw earlier in the book, but who is this harlot he's describing? One thing we know is that she is sitting on top of a scarlet colored beast with seven heads and ten horns. This is the same beast we saw earlier coming out of the sea (1st beast), this time he is described as being scarlet in color. Scarlet is the color of royalty; we already know that the beast represents the world's kingdoms; here we also see that these kingdoms rule over the world.

The woman (the great whore) is also dressed in purple and scarlet, adorned with gold, precious stones and pearls. She has on the attire of a queen; wearing the garments of royalty. This queen who is ruling the kingdoms of the world is drunk with the blood of the saints (Old Testament) and the martyrs of Jesus (the Church). The last verse of Revelation chapter 17 gives us more insight into this woman's identity.

*Revelation 17:18 And **the woman which thou sawest is that great city**, which reigneth over the kings of the earth.*

The woman is also described as the great city that rules over the kingdoms of the earth. What do we know about the scarlet colored beast (1st beast)? We know that it represents the kingdoms of this world and that each head represents a different kingdom. The only kingdom to really be singled out by John was the Roman Empire. Let's assume that for now that we are still referring to the Roman Empire, then the great city (the woman) would be Rome.

Rome was the capital of the empire, so the picture of the woman on top of the beast would definitely fit. Rome was also responsible for killing Jews (the destruction of Jerusalem) and Christians. If Rome is the great city mentioned, why is she also proclaimed as the great whore? First of all Rome is likened to Babylon (worldliness) and the city is being contrasted to Jerusalem. The city's (Rome) forehead is imprinted with the words, "Mystery, Babylon the Great, the Mother of harlots and of the abominations of the earth". Let's look at Jerusalem to gain understanding into what John is attempting to convey to us.

> *Galatians 4:26 But **Jerusalem** which is above is free,*
> ***which is the mother of us all.***

In the fourth chapter of Galatians the apostle Paul is teaching that all believers are children of Jerusalem that is above (New Jerusalem). In contrast everyone that is led by his or her flesh (666), is considered to be a child of Rome/Babylon (2nd Beast) that is below. Remember that the 2nd beast ascended from below the earth. In this instance the word whore means to pursue faithless, unworthy, or idolatrous desires. Therefore Rome is being used in a spiritual sense and she is declared to be the Great whore, the mother of harlots. Rome that is from below is the antithesis of Jerusalem that is from above.

The great harlot destroyed

> **And the ten horns which thou sawest upon the beast, these shall hate the whore, and shall make her desolate and naked, and shall eat her flesh, and burn her with fire.**
> **For God hath put in their hearts to fulfil his will, and to agree, and give their kingdom unto the beast, until the words of God shall be fulfilled.**

> ***Revelation 17:16,17***

The beast's (1st beast) description has changed to he that was and is not. The beast we have established represents the Roman Empire but here we see it comes to an end. This news brings comfort to the churches of Asia and elsewhere, because of the suffering the Empire has brought them. Previously we saw that the seven mountains the woman sits on are the Seven Hills of Rome.

Now we are told that the mountains have a dual meaning, they are also 7 kings. Five have fallen, one is and the last has yet to come. We also know that mountains represent kings or kingdoms, in this case the kings are really kingdoms. The five that have fallen are the Egyptian, Assyrian, Babylonian, Persian/Medes and the Grecian empires. The Roman Empire is the one that is and the Barbarians are the seventh kingdom yet to come and must continue a short time.

1. Egyptian empire.
2. Assyrian empire.
3. Babylonian empire.
4. Persian/Medes empires.
5. Grecian empire.
6. Roman empire.
7. Barbarians.

We have a riddle of sorts before us, "the beast that was, and is not, and yet is, is himself also the eighth (beast), and is of the seven". Who is the beast that was and is not, and yet is?

The Roman Empire is the beast that was and is not, yet is present. Then the Byzantium Empire is the 8th beast, which is part of the original seven. As we saw previously with Noah the number eight represents resurrection. So the eighth kingdom is actually the 6th kingdom (Roman Empire) resurrected. How was the Roman Empire resurrected or brought back to life?

Rome was split in half by the emperor Diocletian in 286 A.D., one half was the Western Empire (based out of Rome) and the other was the Eastern Empire (city of Byzantium).

> **Byzantium** *had first been reconstructed in the time of Septimuis Severus **not just as a Roman city, but modeled on Rome itself, on and around seven hills**. Later Constantine*

the Great chose it as his new capital, renaming it Constantinople, and it remained the capital of the eastern part of the Roman Empire.[47]

Constantinople or Byzantine is a reincarnation or clone of the original Empire's capital Rome. Byzantine is the 8th beast and is of the seven, the Eastern Empire (Byzantine) is in reality the Roman Empire along with the western half.

Next we have the 10 horns which John tells us are 10 kings, that have not received a kingdom yet (as of 96 A.D.). But for one hour will receive authority as kings with the beast (6th head). These kings will make war against the Lamb but the Lamb will overcome them. Daniel gives us more insight into the identity of these 10 horns.

> *Daniel 2:41 And **whereas thou sawest the** feet and **toes**, part of potters' clay, and part of iron, **the kingdom shall be divided**; but there shall be in it of the strength of the iron, forasmuch as thou sawest the iron mixed with miry clay.*

> *Daniel 7:24 And **the ten horns out of this kingdom are ten kings** that shall arise: and **another shall rise after them**; and he shall be diverse from the first, **and he shall subdue three kings**.*
> *Daniel 7:25 **And he shall speak great words against the most High, and shall wear out the saints** of the most High, **and think to change times and laws:** and they shall be given into his hand until a time and times and the dividing of time.*

In the second chapter of Daniel the 10 kings are referred to as toes (ten is implied), in the seventh chapter he calls them horns. Daniel chapter 2 reveals that the beast's kingdom will be divided; we know from history that the empire was split in half by Emperor Diocletian in 286 A.D. We are further told that the 10 horns are ten kings that will rise from the empire with another king conquering 3 of the ten. This little horn will attempt to change laws and seek to change times (calendars) and he will persecute the saints of God. Let's look at some more historical facts to see who exactly are these 10 horns.

Hailed emperor on 20 November AD 284, immediately, or shortly after this execution, Gaius Aurelius Valerius Diocletian - the name he assumed with the imperial title - crossed the Bosporus into Europe and met the forces of Numerian's brother and co-emperor Carinus at Margum on 1 April AD 285.

Diocletian was in fact losing the battle as the assassination of Carinus by one of his own officers, left the opposing army without a leader. With only one imperial candidate still left on the field, Carinus' army surrendered accepting Diocletian as emperor. Carinus' murder would also suggest a possible involvement by **Diocletian**, connecting him (although solely by rumor) **with the possible assassination of three emperors.**

Under Diocletian the imperial court was much expanded and elaborated. People were to kneel before their emperor, kissing the hem of his robes. All this was no doubt introduced to yet further increase the authority of the imperial office. Under Diocletian the emperor became a god-like creature, detached from worldly affairs of the lesser people around him.

But **Diocletian**, the great reformer of the empire, **should also become known for a very harsh persecution of the Christians**. Trying to strengthen Roman traditions, he much revived worship of the old Roman gods.[48]

In about the year 530 A.D., there lived a monk named Dionysius Exiguus - "Denis the Little" - from Scythia in southwest Russia. Like many scholars at the time, Dionysius was concerned with the correct calculation of the date of Easter, and he constructed a table of Easter dates for a nineteen-year period which he designated Anni Domini Jesu Christi 532-550.

At the time, years were measured from the beginning of the reign of the emperor Diocletian, two-and-a-half centuries earlier. Dionysius had decided, through careful calculation, that **Anno Diocletiani** (the original meaning of A.D.) 248 was 532 years since the birth of Jesus Christ. And since Easter commemorates the most important event in the Christian faith, **Dionysius believed that it was inappropriate to date the years by the reign of one of the most notorious persecutors that the Church had ever known.**[49]

History bears out that Diocletian is the little horn referred to in the book of Daniel. Now we can easily identify the 10 horns described in Daniel and Revelation. I have omitted Diocletian (286-305 A.D.) from the list since the little horn is in addition to the ten.

1. Carus 282-283 A.D. - defeated by Diocletian.
2. Numerian 283-284 A.D. - defeated by Diocletian.
3. Carinus 283-285 A.D. - defeated by Diocletian.
4. Maximian 286-305 A.D.
5. Carausius 287-293 A.D.

6. Constantius I 305-306 A.D.
7. Severus II 306-307 A.D.
8. Maxentius 306-312 A.D.
9. Maximian (returned) 307-308 A.D.
10. Constantine 307-337 A.D.

There were many famous rulers over the Roman Empire, so why are these ten emperor's singled out in scripture? The empire historically has had rulers that persecuted the church but in these 10 emperors a major shift will take place. Remember before we said that these kings will make war against the Lamb but the Lamb will overcome them. The war with the Lamb is the persecution of His church but God did not launch a physical battle against the empire, instead through the church (fervent prayer) he instigated a spiritual one.

Constantine (the 10th horn) claimed to have had a vision on the way to Rome, during the night before battle. In this dream he supposedly saw the 'Chi-Ro', the symbol of Christ, shining above the sun. Seeing this as a divine sign, it is said that Constantine had his soldiers paint the symbol on their shields. Following this Constantine went on to defeat the numerically stronger army of Maxentius at the Battle at the Milvian Bridge (Oct AD 312). Constantine saw this victory as directly related to the vision he had the night before.

Henceforth Constantine saw himself as an emperor of the Christian people. If this made him a Christian is the subject of some debate. But Constantine, who only had himself baptized on his deathbed, is generally understood as the first Christian emperor of the Roman world.[50]

Through Constantine Christianity spread throughout the empire and subsequently became the state religion of Rome. So instead of Satan crushing the church through the beast, the empire itself began to propagate the gospel message throughout the world. This is how the Lamb overcame the 10 horns and the beast.

Ultimately God will destroy the Great Harlot and burn her with fire, and then she will have been recompensed for her sins. Except for the destruction of the Great Harlot this vision really belongs in the "Present" segment of the book. The ten horns have a dual meaning just like the 7 heads represent physical hills and kingdoms. The horns represent not only kings but also kingdoms or countries, which were part of the old Empire. So ten unidentified countries will destroy the great city (Rome) in the future. The Empire has been gone for years, so why would any country need to fight against Rome?

One last vestige of the empire still exists today in Rome, the church, but without the power of its former years. Why would God want to destroy the Roman Catholic Church? Because as we stated earlier it is the 2nd beast (false prophet), that is connected to the 1st beast (Roman Empire). The origin, doctrine and the deeds of the Catholic Church are clearly established and documented. The historical accounts can be freely accessed, so there is no need for me to elaborate on them here.

It is not my aim to condemn the Catholic Church; I have only highlighted the areas that pertain to the Empire itself. The church has done many good and needful things and there are of course many sincere and devout people in the Catholic faith today. I am only pointing out the history and practices of the church as they relate to the book of Revelation. You can judge for yourself whether or not the Roman church is the 2nd beast described by John.

So if the Catholic Church is the false prophet, then why didn't God destroy Rome and the church when the empire fell? One reason for not destroying Rome immediately was that the Roman Catholic Church was the main agent for publishing the gospel throughout the empire and the world. John's Revelation gives us spiritual insight allowing us to see that the Empire was being steered by the dragon (Satan) and we know that the Empire heavily influenced the Catholic Church. In spite of these facts God was still able to use them as a vehicle to spread His gospel.

Before we get the wrong impression and think that our religion is okay, remember that organized religion is man made and therefore falls far short of God's holy standard. In fact religions in general are plagued with fallacies and schisms but God still uses them to publish His gospel and to fulfill His will in the earth. This points to the power and wisdom of God, not the legitimacy of our individual religions.

In 70 ad. Israel was surrounded by the Roman Army and was destroyed, God allowed the Empire to be an instrument of punishment for the Jews. This time around the Lord will visit the many sins of Rome by destroying the city and make her totally desolate. God is not interested in destroying the Catholic Church per se but He is making a powerful statement by judging the city for her many sins. Remember that Rome is symbolic for the world's system, so by destroying the city, God is physically demonstrating a spiritual reality. The world's kingdoms will be judged (destroyed) and the kingdom of God will stand forever.

Chapter 25

Babylon the Great
(Revelation 18-19:6)

For all nations have drunk of the wine of the wrath of her fornication, and the kings of the earth have committed fornication with her, and the merchants of the earth are waxed rich through the abundance of her delicacies.
And I heard another voice from heaven, saying, Come out of her, my people, that ye be not partakers of her sins, and that ye receive not of her plagues.

Revelation 18:3,4

Babylon the Great and the woman (the Great City) are one and the same. John spends a lot of time describing the destruction of Babylon, the 17th, 18th and part of the 19th chapter of Revelation are dedicated to it. Why is this city and its kingdom singled out and given so much attention? Rome and her empire are responsible for centuries of persecution and killings. The followers of Judaism and Christianity have suffered greatly at the hands of the empire and her church. God must act in accordance to His Word; there must be retribution for her many offenses.

Revelation 18:5 For her sins have reached unto heaven, and God hath remembered her iniquities.
Revelation 18:6 Reward her even as she rewarded you, and double unto her double according to her works: in the cup which she hath filled fill to her double.

For this reason, God tells His people to come out of her, before we share in her sins and receive her punishment. Like most things that pertain to Christ there is a duality in this admonition, this is both a physical and spiritual warning. Physically we are told to flee this city because of the impending destruction that is coming to it. The same warning was given to the Church before the destruction of Jerusalem in 70 AD. More importantly we are told to flee Rome in the spiritual sense, for she represents Babylon or all that is worldly (666).

Since the Lord tells His people to come out of the Great City, there is a possibility that her physical destruction is before the rapture. If that is the case then all of the visions pertaining to her belong in the previous segment. God has not given me insight into His timetable for this event but He has shared the most important part, "Come out of her". If we heed this warning and do not receive the mark of the beast, then we will be saved both physically and spiritually.

Lastly we see when Rome is burned, that she will be completely destroyed. In the past the city was always able to rebuild but this time the eternal city will be no more. The Lord will bring her to utter ruin beyond repair and His judgment will stand. When this great city will be destroyed is unknown but we have been warned of God not to take part in her sins. This is a warning to Christian and non-Christian alike, hear what the Spirit of the Lord is saying today.

The earth mourns Babylon

> **And the kings of the earth, who have committed fornication and lived deliciously with her, shall bewail her, and lament for her, when they shall see the smoke of her burning.**
>
> **Standing afar off for the fear of her torment, saying, Alas, alas, that great city Babylon, that mighty city! for in one hour is thy judgment come.**

Revelation 18:9,10

Before we start to think that the only kingdoms or world powers that fit the description of the beast are ancient. A quick survey of the world today would reveal that the United States is a better fit for Babylon than Rome. We must remember that Rome is being used primarily as a symbolic example of the beast, as well as a literal one.

America was initially formed upon Christian principles and practices but we have strayed from the original foundation of our nation. Just turn on a television to preview the current state of our country's moral condition. Sex and violence permeate every sector; talk shows, dramas, sitcoms, the nightly news and even cartoons have been affected. Just because churches litter our landscape does not make us a Christian nation. It just means that we're religious, which in a sense is a step above being superstitious.

Revelation is God's final message to his creation and the reoccurring theme is repentance. We need to evaluate where we stand with God and then make changes to our lives accordingly. We all need to improve in some area of our lives, it's said that the largest room is the room for improvement. I'm not talking about becoming a religious zealot or fanatic but rather a God centered person of integrity. This is what the Lord is looking for in His creation.

Micah 6:8 **He hath shewed thee**, *O man, what is good; and* **what doth the LORD require** *of thee, but to do justly, and to love mercy, and to walk humbly with thy God?*

1. Do Justly - do what is right.
2. Love mercy - be forgiving and tolerant of others.
3. Humbly walk with God - honor God in everything you do.

That's it in a nutshell; salvation is beautiful in its simplicity but religion, well that's a different story. Following these 3 simple things will bring immediate benefits in your physical, mental and emotional health. It will improve your relationships with family, friends and co-workers. In fact if you follow them faithfully they will revolutionize your life I guarantee it, better than that God Himself guarantees it.

Remember when we focus on Babylon or Rome what we're really talking about is the system that rules the world. The world's system revolves around money but God clearly states that you cannot serve Him and money. Your true allegiance can only be to one or the other. This is what the Lord is referring to when He says that the kings of the earth have committed fornication with the whore. They have compromised (violated) themselves for the gain of money and possessions at the expense of their souls.

Mark 8:36 **For what shall it profit a man, if he shall gain the whole world, and lose his own soul?**

Matthew 6:24 No man can serve two masters: for either he will hate the one, and love the other; or else he will hold to the one, and despise the other. **Ye cannot serve God and mammon.**

God's system is diametrically opposed to that of the worlds'. God says give and it will be given to you, the world says hold on to what you have. The Lord says esteem your fellow man above yourself, the world says look out for number one. The golden rule has been replaced it is no longer "do unto others as you want them to do unto you" but it's "do unto others before they do it to you".

God wants His people happy and prosperous, as humans we need material things for our benefit and enjoyment. God provides for His people and wants us to have possessions but it's when we allow our possessions to have us, we have erred (sinned). If our thoughts are only on me and mine, then we have stepped out of harmony with the Lord. Everything in life needs balance; the Christian walk is no different.

The earth mourns Babylon for selfish reasons because she has brought them riches and prosperity. Notice they stand far off and watch the destruction they don't get involved. Nowhere do you see that anyone tries to rescue Babylon from her dreaded fate. If America were to collapse how would that impact society and what affect would that have on the world's economy? Truly the world's merchants would mourn such a tragedy because the ramifications would be immense.

Why is so much attention given to Babylon's destruction? Retribution is not what God truly wants; His goal is to remove our illegitimate desires, so that we can finally turn to Him. In America we live in a land of great luxury and freedom, it is easy to become self absorbed, materialistic and indifferent. We have a tendency to look at salvation and repentance as encumbering commandments, which cramp our lifestyle. In reality salvation is God reaching out to us in love and repentance is accepting His love by taking hold of His hand. We see salvation as restrictive but in reality it is the only way we can experience true freedom.

Heaven rejoices over Babylon

Rejoice over her, *thou* heaven, and *ye* holy apostles and prophets; for God hath avenged you on her.

And a mighty angel took up a stone like a great millstone, and cast *it* into the sea, saying, Thus with violence shall that great city Babylon be thrown down, and shall be found no more at all.

Revelation 18:20,21

Here we see a is a sharp contrast in the reaction to Babylon's demise, the earth mourns the loss of her but heaven rejoices over it. As much as God wants to bring His creation to repentance, there is still a great need for punishment. If there are no ramifications to man's sins, then He will commit even greater sins.

This is a major problem today because we live in the period called grace; people actually think there is no penalty for their wrongdoing. Man is fickle in this respect because if God punished us immediately for each wrong deed, then we would say that He is too severe. But since He doesn't react right away to every offense, we think that we have gotten away with something and we do even more wrong. Those who have children can readily identify with this pattern of behavior.

> *2 Peter 3:9* ¶ ***The Lord is not slack concerning his promise***, *as some men count slackness;* ***but is longsuffering to us-ward***, *not willing that any should perish, but* ***that all should come to repentance***.

Because those who do evil seem to prosper and even flourish many believe that God either doesn't care or doesn't exist. It is only because of His great love for us that we are not consumed in His anger. As the Bible says, "do not be fooled God is not mocked, whatever a man sows he will reap"[51]. Heaven rejoices because God has finally brought justice to His saints that have patiently endured hardship (tribulation) from obeying His Word. The earth mourns for selfish reasons (loss of revenue) but heaven rejoices in the righteousness of God's judgment.

The great multitude is heard rejoicing and praising God for His righteous judgments against the Great Whore. They are heard and not seen, this could be another hint that the destruction of Babylon occurs before the rapture. Caution: Do not use the destruction of Rome as a sign of the rapture. If it occurs before the wrath of God is poured out, then it will probably occur almost simultaneously. Remember some catastrophic event must occur, in order to rationalize the disappearance of the church. Otherwise everyone would repent and we have seen through John's prophecy that is not the case.

Chapter 26

The Battle of Armageddon
(Revelation 19:11-21)

And I saw heaven opened, and behold a white horse; and he that sat upon him *was* called Faithful and True, and in righteousness he doth judge and make war.

His eyes *were* as a flame of fire, and on his head *were* many crowns; and he had a name written, that no man knew, but he himself.

And he *was* clothed with a vesture dipped in blood: and his name is called The Word of God.

Revelation 19:11-13

This passage of scripture is often mistakenly referred to as the Second Coming of Christ. These verses describe what we saw when the sixth bowl was poured out. This is yet another description of the battle of Armageddon, at this point Christ has already returned to earth though not physically. Christ will only return in bodily form in the New Heaven and Earth, not during the battle of Armageddon or the millennial reign.

The armies of heaven following the Lord are those who were included in the 1st resurrection. They are arrayed in fine white linen, which represents the righteous acts of the saints of God. They now stand in judgment of the world with Christ as He administers the justice of God.

The beast and the false prophet are captured and thrown in to the lake of fire. Since the beast and the false prophet are not physical beings, we cannot interpret this as a literal event. The intention here is that the great world powers and the false religions that support them will collapse and be destroyed forever. Those who are still alive will to be killed with the sword (judgment) from the mouth of Christ; this is figurative for the Word of God. The Lord is not physically fighting but this war is representative of His judgment against the nations.

Judgment waits for all that have the mark of the world (666); God's punishment has been stored up for this climatic event. Notice John states that those who received the mark have been deluded. In other words everyone who chose not to accept Christ has been conned or duped. To think that living your life apart from God is worth the eternal consequences of hell (2nd death) is an immense mistake to say the least. God has instituted one major principle in the earth that affects all life; it decrees that whatever you sow you will reap.

It touches all things and nothing is exempt from it, the concept is simple yet profound. Every culture has a variation of this principle in one form or another, because it is a fundamental law of life. This is why the soul that sinneth shall die; if you sow to the flesh (sin) you will reap death, because sin separates you from God. The Word will condemn all that reject Christ and His gospel; this is the second death. The first death is physical and the second is spiritual, the first is temporal but the second is eternal.

One of the most anticipated conflicts of all time is the battle of Armageddon. This will be the war to end to end all wars, the last and final conflict. The book of Ezekiel calls this battle God's sacrificial meal, while Revelation describes it as the supper of the great God. Obviously there is a lot more to this than a dispute over land. The Lord declares that through this war, *I will set my glory among the heathen, and all the heathen shall see my judgment that I have executed, and my hand that I have laid upon them. So the house of Israel shall know that I am the LORD their God from that day and forward.*[52]

This scripture implies that Israel will turn their hearts and receive the salvation of the Lord (Jesus Christ). The apostle Paul stated this way, *And they also, if they abide not still in unbelief, shall be grafted in: for God is able to graft them in again. For if thou were cut out of the olive tree which is wild by nature, and were grafted contrary to nature into a good olive tree: how much more shall these, which be the natural branches, be grafted into their own olive tree? For I would not, brethren, that ye should be ignorant of this mystery, lest ye should be wise in your own conceits; that blindness in part is happened to Israel, until the fullness of the Gentiles be come in. And so all Israel shall be saved: as it is written, There shall come out of Sion the Deliverer, and shall turn away ungodliness from Jacob.*[53]

Today the Jews adamantly reject Jesus as the Messiah but in the future some decisive event will alter that conclusion. Maybe it's the rapture or possibly the battle of Armageddon but whatever the stimulus is God will use it to restore the Jews, keeping His covenant with the Old Testament patriarchs. When Israel's enemies surround her, God will stand up and fight for her, just like in biblical times. Not because Israel deserves it necessarily but to prove to the nations that He is the Lord of the whole earth. Even in this final act of judgment God is calling the world to repentance.

> **Physically man is fighting over a prized (holy) parcel of land; spiritually the warfare is over the priceless soul of man.**

The spiritual implications of this war far outweigh the physical, because nothing on earth is more valuable than your soul. Armageddon is more than the final global war; it is the climatic battle of good and evil waged over the soul of man. We need to keep in mind that although the decisive battle of Armageddon (the final conflict) is a future event, the war is being fought here and now.

Chapter 27

The Marriage Supper of the Lamb
(Revelation 19:7-10)

Let us be glad and rejoice, and give honour to him: for the marriage of the Lamb is come, and his wife hath made herself ready.

Revelation 19:7

Here John shows us the Lamb preparing to be married. Marriage is a union that should not be broken, the two shall become one, inseparable forever. The question is who is Christ's bride? In 21st chapter of Revelation we are told that the holy city, New Jerusalem is the bride prepared for Christ. Remember that these are not actual or literal events but they are types to help us understand our relationship with the Lord and His Christ.

New Jerusalem is made up of both Israel and the Church; the individuals that comprise both of these entities are considered her children or offspring. So the bride and New Jerusalem are synonymous with the kingdom of God. The church is not the bride but she is a combination of the Israel (144,000) and the church.

In the Jewish tradition the preparation for the bride was one of purification and anticipation. The bride would take what is called a mikveh, which is a bath of purification. Even today, Jewish brides need to obtain a certificate to show that they have acquired the ceremonial mikveh[54].

The time between Jesus' first advent and His second is the bride's time of purification, anticipation and preparation for the groom's return. The mikveh is the washing through the Word and the blood of the Lamb. We are to remain pure to Jesus and not fornicate ourselves to other god's. We are not to commit spiritual infidelity. Spiritual fornication is the act of loving anything or anyone more than God[55]. In other words whatever captures the focus of our time, energy and thoughts becomes our god. We need to always have our priorities in perspective (according to God's Word) to maintain a healthy balance in our lives.

127

This wedding will be a time of great celebration and festivities; there will be joy, singing and dancing. Everyone is invited to join in on the festivities. The voice of the Lord goes throughout the earth and bids us to come; His Spirit is constantly compelling us to draw near.

> *Luke 14:16 Then said he unto him, A certain man made a great supper, and bade many:*
>
> *Luke 14:17 And sent his servant at supper time to say to them that were bidden,* ***Come; for all things are now ready.***
>
> *Luke 14:22 And the servant said, Lord, it is done as thou hast commanded, and yet there is room.*
>
> *Luke 14:23 And the lord said unto the servant, Go out into the highways and hedges, and* ***compel them to come in, that my house may be filled.***

The invitation to salvation has been sent RSVP (the gospel), will you respond or will you miss the event of a lifetime?

Chapter 28

The Great White Throne Judgment
(Revelation 20:11-15)

And I saw a great white throne, and him that sat on it, from whose face the earth and the heaven fled away; and there was found no place for them.

And I saw the dead, small and great, stand before God; and the books were opened: and another book was opened, which is *the book* of life: and the dead were judged out of those things which were written in the books, according to their works.

Revelation 20:11,12

L astly we see the heaven and the earth destroyed before God. Heaven is referring to the skies above the earth, not the throne of God. Every soul is gathered (2nd resurrection) before the Lord, these judgments will both reward the saints and punish the sinners. These rewards and punishments are not simply salvation and damnation, otherwise why would God need to judge our individual works. First your decision to either accept of reject Christ will determine your salvation or damnation, all who accept Christ are recorded in the book of Life. In addition to this your works or actions will determine the amount/degree of your rewards or punishments, this is what the other books contain.

*1 Corinthians 3:13 **Every man's work shall be made manifest**: for the day shall declare it, because it shall be revealed by fire; and the fire shall try every man's work of what sort it is.*

1 Corinthians 3:14 If any man's work abide which he hath built thereupon, he shall receive a reward.

1 Corinthians 3:15 If any man's work shall be burned, he shall suffer loss: but he himself shall be saved; yet so as by fire.

Here Paul is speaking to Christians, so we see it is possible to be saved and yet suffer loss because of our works or lack of them. This is better than being eternally lost but it is certainly not God's best for us. After salvation we must strive to do our best for God and to follow His will completely. Quoting Paul again, *Know ye not that they which run in a race run all, but one receiveth the prize? So run, that ye may obtain.*[56] God is not looking purely at our works or the end result but He sees into every intention and motivation of our actions.

> *Hebrews 4:12 For **the word of God** [is] quick, and powerful, and sharper than any twoedged sword, piercing even to the dividing asunder of soul and spirit, and of the joints and marrow, and [is] **a discerner of the thoughts and intents of the heart.***

God judges the heart or the true intentions of people so while your actions may outwardly appear good the Lord knows your true motives and He will judge you accordingly. Let us go on with the knowledge that nothing that we do will slip pass the Lord, whether it is good or bad so let us do all things as to the Lord. There is one last enemy to be cast into the lake of fire and then all things will be completed, that enemy is death.

> *1 Corinthians 15:24 Then [cometh] the end, when he shall have delivered up the kingdom to God, even the Father; when he shall have put down all rule and all authority and power.*
> *1 Corinthians 15:25 For he must reign, till he hath put all enemies under his feet.*
> *1 Corinthians 15:26 **The last enemy [that] shall be destroyed [is] death.***

Death is referred to as an enemy of God, so obviously it is not God who is responsible for taking our love ones from us. Death came about through man's disobedience (sin) and only through sin can death reign. But God through his kingdom has even subdued this fatal enemy. Anyone, whose name is not found in the book of Life, will be thrown into the lake of fire along with death, Hades, the Devil, the beast and the false prophet. The lake of fire is referred to as the second death, which equates to eternal torment and separation from God.

Since spirits can't experience physical pain the lake of fire cannot be a literal occurrence. The lake of fire illustrates the fact that it is impossible to escape and to highlight the intense torment associated to this state of being. Why suffer in this life and the next, this is one experience that is totally avoidable.

The judgment of the Lord is final, which is why the message of repentance has been repeated constantly throughout the book of Revelation and the Bible itself for that fact. If we refuse to accept God's remedy for sin then we must be willing to suffer the eternal consequences of our actions. Man was created to rule the earth and to experience the fullness and beauty of God, to accept anything less is a tragedy.

Chapter 29

The New Heaven and Earth
(Revelation 21:1-22:5)

M ost of the book of Revelation has been dealing with or alluding to the wrath of God, in one form or another. At this point we shift gears and move past this event to catch a glimpse of the future of mankind.

New Creation

> **And I saw a new heaven and a new earth: for the first heaven and the first earth were passed away; and there was no more sea.**

> *Revelation 21:1*

A new heaven and earth replace the old creation. Again heaven is referring to the sky or the atmosphere, not the dwelling place of God. In the new earth we see that the sea no longer exists; it is a natural boundary between nations. The sea in this instance represents division and separation. The sea is also symbolic of the grave or death; in this passage both references are applicable.

In the new heaven and earth there will no longer be a separation of countries, nations or peoples. There will be one people or brotherhood and they are all under God's dominion in His kingdom. There will no longer be a divisive distinction among people but we will all be children of God. In addition to this, death will be removed from God's new creation, death only came about through man's sin. God will restore things back to the way they were in the beginning before the sin of man. The earth will once again become a paradise, untainted by the devices of men.

New Jerusalem descends

> **And I John saw the holy city, New Jerusalem, coming down from God out of heaven, prepared as a bride adorned for her husband.**
> **And I heard a great voice out of heaven saying, Behold, the tabernacle of God *is* with men, and he will dwell with them, and they shall be his people, and God himself shall be with them, *and be* their God.**

> ### *Revelation 21:2,3*

Here we clearly see the identity of the bride of Christ, the holy city New Jerusalem. Therefore New Jerusalem was specifically made for us to live in. Contrary to popular belief we will not spend eternity in heaven. Heaven is not our aim, goal or final destination but our desire should be to walk with the Lord in the New Jerusalem (paradise restored). Man was created from the earth and for the earth, although man has sinned and destroyed much. No one (Satan or man) can thwart God's eternal purpose for His creation.

Besides the exclusion of the sea another difference is that God's tabernacle (dwelling place) is now with men, instead of in heaven. The invisible realm we call heaven will be physically manifested in the New Earth, specifically the New Jerusalem. We will finally see Him face to face and know Him as we are known. We will no longer wonder if God is listening to our prayers or seeing our needs. We will have direct personal contact with Him at all times. The Lord declares that He will be our God and we will be His sons. We will be included in His family forever; having full access to God, this is truly heaven.

Let me digress for a moment the Word says that we will become sons of God, not sons and daughters. The Bible is not being chauvinistic; the use of gender in scripture has a distinct purpose. Both males and females are considered sons of God, because in the Hebrew (Jewish) tradition as well as others; the female did not inherit anything from the father. She received only from her husband, only the sons were entitled to inherit from their father and even then there was a distinction between the firstborn and the rest. (There were exceptions to this rule see Numbers 27:1-11)

The use of gender here let's us know that all (male and female) will receive the son's portion of the inheritance through Jesus Christ. There are no distinctions between the sexes in God's eyes, he created them equally and he will reward them likewise. There are many more examples of God using gender to confer spiritual truths to us but we cannot go into them here.

Robert R. Davis

In the new creation all of the things that we don't understand, all of the needless suffering, the pain and anguish will be gone. The Word declares that God will wipe every tear from our eyes; the Lord Himself will comfort and cheer us. We may have had great difficulties in this life; tragedies, handicaps and sorrows. Perhaps our love one's remained unsaved. Maybe we are full of sorrow from seeing how much we failed God, when we finally see what we could have accomplished with the resources God has given us.

> **Our Father will take away every sorrow from this life and replace it with joy unspeakable.**

It's impossible for words or pictures to describe the true feeling of those who will receive the kingdom of God. Nothing even comes close, so John doesn't even attempt it. This is definitely one of those things that you have to experience for yourself.

New Jerusalem described

> **And there came unto me one of the seven angels which had the seven vials full of the seven last plagues, and talked with me, saying, Come hither, I will shew thee the bride, the Lamb's wife.**

> ***Revelation 21:9***

The holy city is a perfect cube of 12,000 furlongs (1377 miles); the wall is 144 cubits (216 feet) in height. The fact that the whole city is measured indicates that it is consecrated to God, having everything in compliance to God's holy standards (measurements). Earlier when we viewed the 2 witnesses the outer court of the temple was not measure because it was given to the Gentiles to tread under foot (desecration) for 42 months[57]. There are 12 gates with the names of the twelve tribes of Israel. Also there are twelve foundations with the names of the twelve apostles of the Lamb. Again we see Israel and the church representing New Jerusalem.

There's no sun or moon for the Lord and His Christ will replace these. God Himself will give illumination to the city and its inhabitants. The inference being that the true knowledge of God will shine upon every citizen of the kingdom, eliminating any chance for deception. The streets are paved in pure transparent gold; this should probably be understood as translucent gold. The foundations of the walls are adorned with all kinds of precious stones and each gate is one large pearl. Whether all of this is a literal or figurative picture, it will be beautiful beyond compare. There will be no more night in the city, because darkness symbolizes sin. Only the people whose names are in the Lamb's book of Life can enter the holy city, Satan and all those who received the mark of the beast are excluded. This is truly paradise restored, man ruined the earth through his sin but now all things are made new through Christ.

There is a pure river of water of life flowing directly from the throne of God and the Lamb. This never-ending continuous flow of water from God will forever refresh and satisfy the needs of man, it is symbolic of the Spirit of God. There are also 2 trees in the city, just like the Garden of Eden but this time there is no tree of knowledge of good and evil. It has been replaced with a second tree of life, which is a numeric allusion to Christ (2nd in the Godhead) being the true source of our eternal life. This time there is no chance to repeat the same mistakes of Eden. Therefore sin and death will never be a part of God's new creation.

If you ever wished things could be the way they once were or felt in your heart that there must be something better for man than this present world. Then make it your goal to enter into the kingdom of God. Only those who overcome the power of Satan and the world (his kingdom) will be allowed to experience the joys of New Jerusalem. The Lord has prepared a glorious new city for His people, even better than the Garden of Eden. I believe as Paul has said, "that these present sufferings shall not compare to the glory that God has prepared for us."[58]

If you want to taste all that God has for you, then make sure your name is written in the Lamb's book of life.

Robert R. Davis

Summary

John's Conclusion
(Revelation 22:6-21)

> **And he said unto me, These sayings *are* faithful and true: and the Lord God of the holy prophets sent his angel to shew unto his servants the things which must shortly be done.**
>
> **Behold, I come quickly: blessed *is* he that keepeth the sayings of the prophecy of this book.**

Revelation 22:6,7

Here at the conclusion of Revelation John repeats the blessing from the opening. After going through the book we now know the specifics of these blessings. Note that the words of this prophecy are not to be sealed, as was the book of Daniel. This book may not be sealed but it has certainly proved to be a real challenge to understand it. Only by the Spirit of God can we even hope to comprehend its meaning.

John states that all of the things shown must shortly come to pass. Yet almost 2000 years have passed and still we are waiting, this shows the patience and longsuffering of God, for he has given us ample time to turn to Him. The gospel has been spread throughout the world, giving us the opportunity to become sons of God.

In the Holy City we see that only the saints can enter but outside are dogs, sorcerers, murders and the like (those who bore the mark of the beast). We see here the implication of the walls around the city. Why else would the kingdom of God need to be walled? Walls are used as a defense, a protection to keep unwanted visitors out. Evidently those who received the mark are on the outside but God has implemented a perimeter that they cannot pass through. So they can see the holy city but they can never enter it.

> *Luke 13:28* **There shall be weeping and gnashing of teeth, when ye shall see Abraham, and Isaac, and Jacob, and all the prophets, in the kingdom of God, and you [yourselves] thrust out.**
>
> *Luke 13:29 And they shall come from the east, and [from] the west, and from the north, and [from] the south, and shall sit down in the kingdom of God.*
>
> *Luke 13:30 And, behold, there are last which shall be first, and there are first which shall be last.*

When you die your spirit lives on but a spirit cannot feel physical pain. So the flames of hell can't, possibly affect Satan or those with the mark. Hell will be seeing God's people basking in the Lord's glory inside the Holy City, and not being able to enter or join them. It's facing the regrets of a life ill spent or from ignoring the message of the gospel and rejecting Christ. Hell is seeing those you laughed at enjoying the presence of God and finding yourself forever excluded. Hell is being constantly reminded that you blew it, it is forever saying if I had only listened. Haven't you ever regretted something in your life and wished you could do it differently, that's torture. Having that remorse forever, that's hell (torment).

Revelation is the only book in the Bible with a warning to anyone that either adds or takes away from its contents. This stresses the significance of this particular prophecy to God. If God places that much importance on the contents of this book, then we would do well to study it prayerfully and carefully.

The Lord Jesus Himself signifies that these words are true, sent by His angel (John). Let him who is thirsty come and take freely of the water of life. This is a personal invitation from Jesus to receive salvation (eternal life), don't ignore it. The Lord's final recorded words are "Surely I am coming quickly", to that John replies "Amen. Even so, come Lord Jesus!" This coming of the Lord involves much suffering but the end is glorious. God has placed before us both blessings and curses, the decision is yours alone which will you choose? If you accept the gospel (Christ) then incomparable blessings and paradise awaits you. If you choose to reject or ignore Him, then you will have all of eternity to relive that decision.

Overview

The Old Testament spring and autumn feasts provide a perfect overview for the book of Revelation. Israel celebrated 6 separate observances that God ordained in the Old Testament. The spring feasts are representative of the Old Testament era and the autumn feasts are indicative of the New Testament. Let's look at the feasts individually to gain a better understanding of their relationship to the book of Revelation.

The Spring Feast:

    Passover and Unleavened Bread
    Firstfruits
    Feast of Weeks

Passover (Feast of Unleavened Bread) celebrates Y'tziat Mitzraim, the Israelite's exodus from Egypt; it is the pivotal event in Jewish history. It freed Israel from more than 200 years of slavery and defined them as a nation[59]. The blood of a spotless lamb was applied to the doorpost of the home and the death angel passed over (bypassed) that particular house.

The sacrifice of the Passover lamb foreshadows Jesus Christ's death on the cross. It is the central and pivotal point in human history. All who accept Christ's sacrifice are freed from the slavery of sin and are now considered citizens of the kingdom of God. When the blood of Christ is applied to door of our hearts, the penalty of death (eternal separation) no longer applies to us but we receive eternal life.

The **Firstfruits** celebration is always observed on the first day of the week during Passover. It is actually part of the festival of unleavened bread (Passover) but God singles it out as a separate observance. The firstfruits of the harvest could not be accepted without first using the male lamb without blemish as a wave offering.

The firstfruits foreshadow the resurrection of Jesus and the 144,000 sealed of God. Jesus rose from the grave on the first day of the week, in accordance to the law of the firstfruits. As we know Jesus represents the lamb without blemish (sin), our sacred Passover and eternal offering before God. As we stated before the firstfruits are presented to God in the temple, this is why the Old Testament saints were seen going into Jerusalem after their resurrection.

The **Feast of Weeks** (Pentecost) was to be observed on the day after the seventh Sabbath—the seven full weeks (seven Sabbaths) from the presentation of the firstfruits. Further, it was to be observed 50 days from the presentation of firstfruits[60]. To the Jews Pentecost commemorates the law given from Mt. Sinai on the fiftieth day out of Egypt.

To the church Pentecost represents the day God wrote the law upon the hearts of men via the Holy Spirit. This celebration represents the new covenant that God has made with Israel and all of mankind, after He delivered us from our spiritual Egypt (sin); it also marks the beginning of the church.

The Autumn Feasts:
Feast of Trumpets
Day of Atonement
Feast of Tabernacles

The **Feast of Trumpets** (Rosh Hashanah) is unique because it is both serious and festive. It is a customary time of spiritual renewal through prayer and deep personal reflection. Jewish tradition states that this observance was to warn the people of the impending Day of Atonement, which came nine days later. It is also the realization that our behavior toward God and each other is literally weighed, judged and ultimately sealed at the close of Yom Kippur (Day of Atonement). According to the Jewish sages there are 3 key elements to insure a good decree from the Lord[61].

- Teshurah (repentance)
- Tfiloh (prayer)
- Tzedakah (charity or love)

Rosh Hashanah correlates to the 7 trumpets in Revelation. On the festive side we have the believers reigning with Christ for a 1000 years, enjoying their newfound liberation and authority in Him. Conversely we have the 7 trumpets warning us of the impending wrath of God to come, urging us to repent. Knowing that we will all have to give an account to God for our every word and deed. Not because God is some kind of sadistic taskmaster but because of the eternal principles on which He founded the world. The laws of sowing and reaping apply not only to the earth but also to man because he was created out of the ground.

The long period between the spring and autumn feasts correlates to the time between start of the church (Pentecost) and the 7th trumpet (the full harvest). The kingdom of God (church) was planted by Jesus and has been growing steadily, at the appropriate time Christ will harvest (rapture) his kingdom from the earth.

The **Day of Atonement** (Yom Kippur) was the day when Israel was to be cleansed of sin. The purpose of killing an innocent animal was not solely to blame it for the collective sins of the people. It was used as a vehicle through which one could transport those sins and transgressions far away. Divine forgiveness was only possible after the entire congregation acknowledged and sought forgiveness for their behavior. This day was the only day on which the ministry of the high priest came in direct contact with the Ark of the Covenant (the mercy seat). At no other time was the ark to be seen by human eyes[62].

The Day of Atonement is symbolic of the rapture of the kingdom of God; the church having its sins forgiven will be counted holy because of the blood and ministry of Christ. Remember that after the 7th trumpet was sounded the Ark of the Covenant was seen in heaven. This indicated that Christ as our high priest finished the work of cleansing the temple (our bodies) and the people of God have received full atonement. All who have not received atonement (1st resurrection) will suffer the wrath of God.

Lastly the **Feast of Tabernacles** (Sukkot) marks the end of a long harvest, it's the time of year when farmers finish their work. To celebrate their hard work, the farmers and their families would go to the temple in Jerusalem to offer thanks. They built sukkot, or booths, to remember how the children of Israel built booths in the desert. The pilgrims lived in them for seven days in Jerusalem, while they and their families celebrated. The closing assembly was the 8th day and the conclusion of the feast.

This festival corresponds to the gathering of all God's people in the New Jerusalem, celebrating and resting from all of their former earthly labors. Everyone who has not received the mark of the beast (overcomers) will be found rejoicing with God in His kingdom. This is the promised time of reaping and enjoying the fruits (rewards) of our labor for the Lord. This is the blessed rest and time of peace that has was prophesied long ago in the scriptures. The reference to the closing assembly on the 8th day refers to our bodies that will finally be redeemed (the old Adamic nature) by Christ; remember the number eight symbolizes resurrection. We will be clothed in our glorious new bodies, just like Jesus our elder brother. Behold all things are become new; this is paradise restored and the end of our long pilgrimage.

Revelation has given us the privilege to have a behind the scenes view of the whole history of man. In addition from observing the various Old Testament feasts we can see that nothing has happened by chance, but God has thoughtfully planned and provided for our salvation. We have the choice to accept or reject what God has freely given to us.

We have seen from this short journey through Revelation, that the Lord has taken great measures to show us his love. By providing us with the choice of salvation, allowing us the ultimate decision over our own destinies. Through Christ we have the ability to cross over the bridge of salvation into the kingdom of God or we can remain where we are.

The central theme of Revelation is repentance, which is critical to salvation. Salvation is God reaching out to mankind; religion is man's attempt to reach up to God. Salvation is pure and simple with very few regulations. Religion on the other hand can be complicated and full of rules. Salvation unifies everyone into the brotherhood of God; it breaks down the walls of separatism. Religion aspires to unify people of like beliefs, but normally results in building more walls in the process. Religion obligates us to make converts of others but salvation motivates (through compassion) us to lead others to Christ. Religion is the proverbial tower of Babel; it is man's attempt to reach heaven through his own efforts.

Should we abandon our individual churches and religions in order to accept God's plan of salvation? Absolutely not, but we need to see the difference between the two and to more importantly keep them in their proper perspectives. Salvation originated from God, religion came from man. The Bible teaches us to trust only in God, because man will disappoint us. We need to clearly see that religion is man made and it will inevitably fail us from time to time. God however will never fail us but if we don't separate religion from God we will wrongly blame Him for the shortcomings of our religion.

Since we know the origin of both salvation and religion, how does religion fit in? Religion should not be viewed as salvation but rather an expression of our collective voice to God in response to salvation. For example the purpose of a car is to take you from point A to point B. Provided that all things are equal as far as reliability and durability, we could conceivably all drive the same type of car. Since the real purpose behind the car is to go from one place to another, everyone's car could be identical but they're not. Even if all things were equal between the vehicles, we would still drive different types of cars. A car does more than transport us to our destinations, it expresses who we are and makes a statement about our personal style or taste.

In the same way our individual religions <u>should</u> only express our personal style of worship. We must remember that religions and our churches are not an end unto themselves. Salvation should the primary objective of religion and no religion on earth can save a person from sin. <u>Religion can only point you to the way but it is not the way</u>. God does not advocate any religion (Baptist, Catholic, Protestant, etc) he only endorses His Son. So when we hear the message of repentance echoed throughout Revelation and the Bible, we must eliminate the added religious connotations from it. There has been so much baggage added to what repentance really is that the very word turns many people off.

God has prepared a glorious kingdom that is equivalent to the paradise of Eden restored and He wants you to enjoy it with Him, free of the negative effects of sin and evil that are in this present world. **Repentance is simply acknowledging what God has done and accepting His gift (Salvation).** There is nothing negative about the act of repentance. We are all in need of salvation, if you haven't already done so I implore you on Jesus' behalf repent today.

> *Romans 10:9 That if thou shalt **confess with thy mouth** the Lord Jesus, and shalt **believe in thine heart** that God hath raised him from the dead, **thou shalt be saved**.*

I hope that this book has blessed you with a fuller understanding of Revelation and the true intent of this final message from God. If you are not ready to meet the bridegroom (Christ) then get ready and if you're already prepared, then resolve to overcome until the end. To close I can only echo the words of John, "the Lord is coming shortly, Amen. <u>Even so, come Lord Jesus</u>".

Robert R. Davis

References

[1] Holy Bible. James 4:14.
[2] Nee, Watchman. Aids to Revelation. (New York: Christian Fellowship Publishers, Inc., 1983) p. 59.
[3] Nee. Aids to Revelation. p. 64.
[4] Holy Bible. Revelation 17:15.
[5] Holy Bible. St. John 4:24.
[6] Holy Bible. Romans 3:23.
[7] Holy Bible. Revelation 5:6
[8] "Knowledge." American Heritage Dictionary. 4th edition 2000.
[9] Nee. Aids to Revelation. p. 60.
[10] Holy Bible. Romans 6:23.
[11] Holy Bible. Ekeziel 18:4.
[12] Holy Bible. Revelation 1:20.
[13] Nee. Aids to Revelation. p. 57.
[14] "Tribulation." American Heritage Dictionary.
[15] Holy Bible, St. Mark 15:25.
[16] Holy Bible, St. Mark 15:34-37.
[17] Holy Bible, St. John 20:1.
[18] Nee. Aids to Revelation. pp. 68,69.
[19] Holy Bible, Hebrews 2:17.
[20] Holy Bible. Romans 16:17
[21] Holy Bible. St. Luke 21:19
[22] Holy Bible. Romans 8:18
[23] Holy Bible. Revelation 22:12.
[24] Holy Bible. St. Luke 9:23.
[25] Global Forest Watch. Frequently Asked Questions. [Online] 23 November 2001. <www.globalforestwatch.org/english/about/faqs.htm >.
[26] American Fisheries Society. American Fisheries Society List Marine Stocks at Risk of Extinction. [Online] 16 November 2000. < http://www.fisheries.org/media/press_releases/pr111600stocks.shtml >.
[27] Bodybuilding. Water the nutrient of Life. [Online] 12 November 2001. < http://bodybuilding.about.com/library/weekly/aa020801a.htm?iam=howstuffworks_ SKD&terms=water >.
[28] Public Interest Research Group. More than 1 in 4 polluters seriously violation clean water permits. [Online] 11 November 2001. < htty: //www pirg org /press/poisonpr html >.
[29] EPA. Air Quality Planning and Standards: John Seitz Regional Haze Testimony. [Online] 28 October 1997. < htt:;// www epa gov/oar./oaqps/JS102897 html >.
[30] Holy Bible. Galatians 5:16.
[31] Holy Bible. St. John 10:10.

[32] "Rome." Encyclopaedia Britannica. 15th edition 1975.

[33] "Rome." Encyclopaedia Britannica Volume.

[34] "Rome." Encyclopaedia Britannica Volume.

[35] "Rome." Encyclopaedia Britannica Volume.

[36] "Rome." Encyclopaedia Britannica Volume.

[37] New American Bible. The Catholic Bible Personal Study Edition. (Oxford University Press, Inc., 1995)

[38] Holy Bible. St. Mark 7:18-20.

[39] Holy Bible. Revelation 20:6.

[40] Nee. Aids to Revelation. p. 67.

[41] Holy Bible. St. Matthew 24:42.

[42] Holy Bible. Revelation 16:5,6.

[43] Environmental Protection Agency. Emissions. [Online] 31 October 2001. < http://www.epa.gov/globalwarming >.

[44] "Generation." Webster's Ninth New Collegiate Dictionary. 1989

[45] Holy Bible. 2 Corinthians 4:4.

[46] Holy Bible. Isaiah 11:1-9 and Isaiah 65:17-25.

[47] The Illustrated History of the Roman Empire. Constantinople. [Online] 14 July 2001. < http://www.Roman-Empire.net/constant/constantinople.html >.

[48] The Illustrated History of the Roman Empire. Decline. [Online] 14 July 2001. < http://www.roman-empire.net/decline/decl-index.html >.

[49] Harper, David. A brief history of the Calendar. [Online] 19 November 1999. <http://www.obliquity.com/calendar/ad.html >.

[50] The Illustrated History of the Roman Empire. Decline.

[51] Holy Bible. Galatians 6:7

[52] Holy Bible. Ezekiel 39:21,22.

[53] Holy Bible. Romans 11:23-26.

[54] New Testament Parallel's. [Online] 20 October 2001. < http://www.geocities.com/heartland/fields/5965/new.htm >.

[55] New Testament Parallel's.

[56] Holy Bible, 1 Corinthians 9:24.

[57] Jamieson, Fausset and Brown. Commentary on the Whole Bible. (Grand Rapids, MI.: Zondervan Publishing House 1962) p. 1588

[58] Holy Bible. Romans 8:18.

[59] Kramer, A. J. Jewish Holidays. [Online] 1999. < http://www.everythingjewish.com/ >.

[60] Kramer, A. J. Jewish Holidays.

[61] Kramer, A. J. Jewish Holidays.

[62] Kramer, A. J. Jewish Holidays.

About the Author

Robert R. Davis has been an ordained deacon for over sixteen years. He has served as Sunday school teacher, youth leader and prison volunteer for many years. He is a spirit-filled believer dedicated to pursuing and sharing the full knowledge of Christ. He and his wife Yvette live in New Haven, Connecticut with their four children, where he continues to write and study the Word of God.

Printed in the United States
4381